Living Language™

CONVERSATIONAL
GERMAN

THE LIVING LANGUAGE™ SERIES
BASIC COURSES ON CASSETTE
  *Spanish
  *French
  *German
  *Italian
  *Japanese
  *Portuguese (Continental)
  Portuguese (South American)
  Advanced Spanish
  Advanced French
  Children's Spanish
  Children's French
  Russian
  Hebrew
  English for Native Spanish Speakers
  English for Native French Speakers
  English for Native Italian Speakers
  English for Native German Speakers
  English for Native Chinese Speakers

*Also available on Compact Disc

LIVING LANGUAGE PLUS®
  Spanish
  French
  German
  Italian

LIVING LANGUAGE TRAVELTALK™
  Spanish
  French
  German
  Italian
  Russian

CONVERSATIONAL
GERMAN

A COMPLETE COURSE
IN EVERYDAY GERMAN

By Genevieve A. Martin

AND

Theodor Bertram

BASED ON THE METHOD DEVISED
BY RALPH WEIMAN, FORMERLY CHIEF OF
LANGUAGE SECTION, U.S. WAR DEPARTMENT

SPECIALLY PREPARED FOR USE WITH
THE LIVING LANGUAGE COURSE IN GERMAN

Crown Publishers, Inc., New York

This work was previously published under the title *Conversation Manual German*.

Copyright © 1956, 1985 by Crown Publishers, Inc.

THE LIVING LANGUAGE COURSE is a registered trademark, and CROWN, and LIVING LANGAGE and colophon are trademarks of Crown Publishers, Inc., 201 East 50th Street, New York, N.Y. 10022.

Library of Congress Catalog Card Number: 56-9319

ISBN 0-517-55781-9

1985 Updated Edition

Manufactured in the United States of America

22   21   20

TABLE OF CONTENTS

INTRODUCTION   XI
INSTRUCTIONS   XIII

**BASIC GERMAN VOCABULARY
AND GRAMMAR**

LESSON 1
1. LETTERS AND SOUNDS   1

LESSON 2
(Sounds II)   2
2. PRONUNCIATION PRACTICE   3

LESSON 3
(Pronunciation Practice I)   5

LESSON 4
(Pronunciation Practice II)   8

LESSON 5
3. THE GERMAN ALPHABET   12
4. BUILDING A VOCABULARY   12

LESSON 6
(General Equivalents)   13
5. USEFUL WORD GROUPS   15

LESSON 7
(Useful Phrases I)   17
6. GOOD MORNING!   17

LESSON 8
(Useful Phrases II)   20
7. DO YOU HAVE...?   20
8. WHAT WILL YOU HAVE TO EAT?   20

LESSON 9
9. COMMON VERB FORMS   22
10. ASKING A QUESTION   25

LESSON 10

    (Nouns, Adjectives)   28
11. THE GERMAN DECLENSION   28
12. THE ARTICLE   29
13. DECLENSION OF NOUNS   29
14. DECLENSION OF ADJECTIVES   32
15. COMPARATIVE AND SUPERLATIVE   34
16. PREPOSITIONS   35

LESSON 11

17. ASKING YOUR WAY   39

LESSON 12

    (Near, Far, There, To Be)   41
18. TO BE OR NOT TO BE   43
19. MY, YOUR, HIS, HER   45

LESSON 13

    (It Is, Questions)   48
20. IT IS, THAT IS   48
21. ASKING A QUESTION   49

LESSON 14

22. TO HAVE AND HAVE NOT   50

LESSON 15

23. SOME WORDS AND IDIOMS   53

LESSON 16

    (Phrases I)   57
24. DO YOU SPEAK GERMAN?   57
25. PLEASE SPEAK A LITTLE SLOWER   58

LESSON 17

    (Phrases II, This, That)   58
26. THANKS   59
27. THIS AND THAT   61

LESSON 18

28. NOT   63
29. NOTHING, NEVER, ETC.   64
30. ISN'T IT?   65
31. I, YOU, HIM   66
32. MYSELF, YOURSELF, HIMSELF   69

LESSON 19
    (Greeting and Leave-Taking)   70
33. HELLO!   70
34. I'D LIKE YOU TO MEET…   71
35. HOW ARE THINGS?   72

LESSON 20
    (Introductions)   74
36. HAVE YOU TWO MET?   74
37. GLAD TO HAVE MET YOU   74

LESSON 21
    (Numbers I)   80
38. NUMBERS   80

LESSON 22
    (Numbers II)   82

LESSON 23
    (Currency, Telephone Numbers, Dates)   85
39. IT COSTS…   85
40. THE TELEPHONE NUMBER IS…   85
41. THE NUMBER IS…   86
42. SOME DATES   86

LESSON 24
    (Time I)   88
43. WHAT TIME IS IT?   88
44. THE TIME IS NOW   90
45. A MATTER OF TIME   91

LESSON 25
    (Time II)   93
46. IT'S TIME   93
47. MORNING, NOON AND NIGHT   94

LESSON 26
    (Time III)   95
48. PAST, PRESENT AND FUTURE   97

LESSON 27
    (Days, Months, Seasons)   98
49. THE DAYS OF THE WEEK   98
50. WHAT'S THE DATE TODAY?   98

51. THE MONTHS   100
52. THE SEASONS   101

LESSON 28
53. TO GO   103
54. A FEW SHORT PHRASES   105

LESSON 29
55. ONE, THEY, PEOPLE   106
56. A LITTLE AND A LOT   109
57. TOO MUCH   111
58. MORE OR LESS   111
59. ENOUGH AND SOME MORE   112
60. GOOD   113
61. GOOD, WELL   113
62. BEAUTIFUL   115
63. LIKE, AS   116
64. ALL, EACH, EVERY   116
65. COMBINATIONS WITH *DAS*   118

LESSON 30
    (Same, Self, Already)   121
66. SMALL TALK   121
67. THE SAME, MYSELF   124
68. ALREADY   125
69. LIKING AND DISLIKING   126

LESSON 31
    (Who, What, Which, How, Why)   133
70. THE INTERROGATIVE PRONOUN   133
71. HOW MUCH?   141
72. HOW MANY?   142

LESSON 32
73. USEFUL WORD GROUPS   144

LESSON 33
74. GETTING AROUND   151

LESSON 34
75. WRITING, PHONING, TELEGRAPHING   153

LESSON 35
   (Family Affairs I)   155
76. FAMILY AFFAIRS   156

LESSON 36
   (Family Affairs II)   158

LESSON 37
77. SHOPPING   164
78. ORDERING BREAKFAST   168
79. A SAMPLE MENU   171

LESSON 38
80. APARTMENT HUNTING   173

LESSON 39
81. TO COME, TO SAY, TO DO   181
82. I'M A STRANGER HERE   188

LESSON 40
   (Conversation)   194
83. THE COMMONEST VERBS   194
84. MEETING AN OLD FRIEND   203
85. THE COMMONEST VERBS (Continued)   209
86. COMMON NOTICES AND SIGNS   219

SUMMARY OF GERMAN GRAMMAR

1. THE ALPHABET   226
2. THE VOWELS   226
3. THE DIPHTHONGS   226
4. THE CONSONANTS   227
5. SPECIAL LETTER COMBINATIONS   228
6. THE GERMAN DECLENSION   228
7. PLURAL OF NOUNS   229
8. GENDER   230
9. THE DEFINITE ARTICLE   232
10. THE INDEFINITE ARTICLE   232
11. THE ADJECTIVES   233
12. COMPARATIVE AND SUPERLATIVE   234
13. THE PARTITIVE   235
14. POSSESSIVE ADJECTIVES   236
15. POSSESSIVE PRONOUNS   237

16.	DEMONSTRATIVE ADJECTIVES	238
17.	DEMONSTRATIVE PRONOUNS	238
18.	RELATIVE PRONOUNS	238
19.	PERSONAL PRONOUN	240
20.	THE INDEFINITE PRONOUN	240
21.	POSITION OF PRONOUNS	241
22.	THE NEGATIVE	241
23.	ADVERBS	241
24.	PREPOSITIONS	244
25.	CONTRACTIONS	245
26.	PREFIXES	245
27.	THE TENSES OF THE INDICATIVE	246
28.	THE PAST PARTICIPLE	248
29.	USE OF THE AUXILIARIES *HABEN* AND *SEIN*	249
30.	THE SUBJUNCTIVE	250
31.	THE CONDITIONAL	251
32.	THE PASSIVE VOICE	252
33.	THE IMPERATIVE	252
34.	THE INFINITIVE	253
35.	COMPLEMENTS OF VERBS	254
36.	CHANGES IN THE NORMAL SEQUENCE OF WORDS WITHIN A SENTENCE	255
37.	INDIRECT DISCOURSE	256
38.	CONSTRUCTION OF THE SENTENCE	257
39.	THE MOST COMMON IRREGULAR VERBS	258
40.	OTHER IRREGULAR VERBS	278

LETTER WRITING

1.	THANK-YOU NOTES	300
2.	BUSINESS LETTERS	301
3.	INFORMAL LETTERS	303
4.	FORMS OF SALUTATIONS AND COMPLIMENTARY CLOSINGS	305
5.	FORM OF THE ENVELOPE	306

INTRODUCTION to the COMPLETE LIVING LANGUAGE COURSE®

The Living Language Course® uses the natural method of language-learning. You learn German the way you learned English—by hearing the language and repeating what you heard. You didn't begin by studying grammar; you first learned how to say things, how words are arranged, and only when you knew the language pretty well did you begin to study grammar. This course teaches you German in the same way. Hear it, say it, absorb it through use and repetition. The only difference is that in this course the basic elements of the language have been carefully selected and condensed into 40 short lessons. When you have finished these lessons, you will have a good working knowledge of the language. If you apply yourself, you can master this course and learn to speak basic German in a few weeks.

While *Living Language™ Conversational German* is designed for use with the complete Living Language Course®, this book may be used without the cassettes. The first 5 lessons cover German pronunciation, laying the foundation for learning the vocabulary, phrases, and grammar that are explained in the later chapters.

All the material is presented in order of importance. When you reach page 150, you will have already learned 300 of the most frequently used sentences and will be able to make yourself understood on many important topics. By the time you have finished this course, you will have a sufficient command of German to get along in all ordinary situations.

The brief but complete summary of German grammar is included in the back of this book to enable you to perfect your knowledge of German. There are also many other helpful features, such as vocabulary tips, practice exercises, and verb charts. The special section on letter-writing will show you how to answer an invitation, make a business inquiry, and address an envelope properly. Just as important is the *Living Language™ Common Usage Dictionary*. This is included in the course primarily for use as a reference book, but it is a good idea to do as much browsing in it as possible. It contains the most common German words with their meanings illustrated by everyday sentences and idiomatic expressions. The basic words—those you should learn from the start—are capitalized to make them easy to find.

Keep practicing your German as much as possible. Once you are well along in the course, try reading German magazines, newspapers, and books. Use your German whenever you get a chance—with German-speaking friends, with the waiter at a German restaurant, with other students.

This course tries to make the learning of German as easy and enjoyable as possible, but a certain amount of application is necessary. The cassettes and books that make up this course provide you with all the material you need; the instructions on the next page tell you what to do. The rest is up to you.

Course Material

The material of the complete Living Language Course® consists of the following:

1. *2 hour-long cassettes.* The label on each face indicates clearly which lessons are contained on that side. (Living German is also available on 4 long-playing records.)

2. *Conversational German book.* This book is designed for use with the recorded lessons, or it may be used alone. It contains the following sections:
    Basic German Vocabulary and Grammar
    Summary of German Grammar
    Verb Charts
    Letter-writing

3. *German-English/English-German Common Usage Dictionary.* A special kind of dictionary that gives you the literal translations of more than 15,000 German words, plus idiomatic phrases and sentences illustrating the everyday use of the more important vocabulary and 1,000 essential words capitalized for ready reference.

How to Use Conversational German with the Living Language™ Cassettes

TO BEGIN
There are 2 cassettes with 10 lessons per side. The beginning of each lesson is announced on the tape and each lesson takes approximately 3 minutes. If your cassette player has a digit indicator, you can locate any desired point precisely.

LEARNING THE LESSONS

1. Look at page 1. Note the words in **boldface** type. These are the words you will hear on the cassette. There are pauses to enable you to repeat each word and phrase right after you hear it.

2. Now read Lesson 1. (The ▭ ▭ symbols indicate the beginning of the recorded material. In some advanced lessons, information and instructions precede the recording.) Note the points to listen for when you play the cassette. Look at the first word: **Albert**, and be prepared to follow the voice you will hear.

3. Play the cassette, listen carefully, and watch for the points mentioned. Then rewind, play the lesson again, and this time say the words aloud. Keep repeating until you are sure you know the lesson. The more times you listen and repeat, the longer you will remember the material.

4. Now go on to the next lesson. It's always good to quickly review the previous lesson before starting a new one.

5. There are 2 kinds of quizzes at the end of each section. One is the matching type, in which you must select the English translation of the German sentence. In the other, you fill in the blanks with the correct German word chosen from the 3 given directly below the sentence. Do these quizzes faithfully and, if you make any mistakes, reread the section.

6. When you get 100 percent on the Final Quiz, you may consider that you have mastered the course.

LESSON 1

1. LETTERS AND SOUNDS

(Letters and Sounds I)

A. Many German sounds are like English. Listen to and repeat the following German names, and notice which sounds are similar and which are different:

Albert	Gustav	Minna
Anton	Hans	Otto
Anna	Heinrich	Paul
Bernhard	Jakob	Paula
Emma	Josef	Richard
Erich	Katharina	Rudolf
Franz	Lotte	Stefan
Friedrich	Ludwig	Thomas
Georg	Martha	Wilhelm

NOTICE:
1. that each sound is pronounced clearly and distinctly; that sounds are not slurred over the way they often are in English.
2. that simple words have one stressed syllable, generally the first one (for your convenience, we have indicated the stress in word study listings for all words with more than one syllable).
3. that the *Umlaut* (¨) is placed at times on the letters *a, o, u,* and changes their pronunciation. Contrast the following examples: *über*—over, *unter*—under.
4. that all nouns are written with a capital letter.

B. Now listen to and repeat the following words which are similar in English and German. Notice how German spelling and pronunciation differ from English:

Adrésse	address
Alphabét	alphabet
Álkohol	alcohol
Amerikáner	American
Bank	bank
Bad	bath
Bett	bed
Bier	beer
Bíschof	bishop
Bútter	butter
Charákter	character
Diréktor	director
Dóktor	doctor
Dráma	drama
Énde	end
Expórt	export
Fábel	fable
Film	film
Garáge	garage
Gas	gas
hier	here
Hotél	hotel
Húnger	hunger
Lámpe	lamp
lang	long

LESSON 2

(Sounds II)

Línie	line
Maschíne	machine
Natión	nation
national	national
Óper	opera
Operétte	operetta
Papíer	paper

Pedál	pedal
Persón	person
parken	(to) park
Prinz	prince
Problem	problem
Públikum	public
Rádio	radio
Restauránt	restaurant
Signál	signal
Statión	station
Telegrámm	telegram
Telefón	telephone
Tee	tea
Theáter	theater
Témpel	temple
Triúmph	triumph
Túnnel	tunnel
Wolf	wolf
Zóne	zone

2. PRONUNCIATION PRACTICE

A. VOWELS

The following groups of words will give you some additional practice in spelling and pronunciation:

ay
1. The sound *a* in the English "ah" or "father":

ságen	to say	Láden	shop
Datum	date	Táfel	board

2. The sound *ä* as in English "fair":

Bär	bear	Währung	currency
Erklärung	declaration	Ernährung	nutrition

3. The sound *e* as in the English "may":

gében	(to) give	**stéhen**	(to) stand
lében	(to) live	**wében**	(to) weave

4. The sound *ee* or *eh* of the English *a* as in "care":

mehr	more	**Heer**	army
leer	empty	**Léhrer**	teacher

5. The sound *e* resembling that of the final English syllable *er* as in "manner":

Eíle	hurry	**hábe**	have!
Adrésse	address	**béte**	pray!

6. The sound *i* as in the English "ship":

Wílle	will	**Schritt**	step
mit	with	**Witz**	joke

7. The sound *o* as in the English "lone":

óben	above	**Bóden**	floor
Obst	fruit	**hólen**	(to) fetch

8. The sound *o* as in the English "love":

oft	often	**Stoff**	material
von	from	**Loch**	hole

9. The sound *ö* is somewhat similar to the German *e* in "*geben*" but with rounded lips:

Kőnig	king	**hőren**	(to) hear
Lőwe	lion	**Mőhre**	carrot

10. The sound *u* like the English *oo* in "room":

nun	now	**Hut**	hat
Blúme	flower	**gut**	good

11. The sound *ü* is rendered by pronouncing the *ee* sound as in the English "see," but with rounded lips:

über	over	**üben**	(to) practice
drüben	over there	**früher**	sooner

12. The same sound is used to pronounce *y*:

týpisch	typical	**Lýrik**	lyrics

LESSON 3

(Pronunciation Practice I)

B. DIPHTHONGS

13. The sounds *ai* and *ei* are always pronounced like the English *y* in "by":

Mai	may	**Ei**	egg
Hai	shark	**Héimat**	homeland

14. The sound *au* is pronounced almost like the English *ou* in "house":

Haus	house	**Baum**	tree
Maus	mouse	**Pfláume**	plum

15. The sounds *äu, eu* are pronounced somewhat
like the English *oy* in "boy":

Häuser	houses	**Leúte**	people
träumen	(to) dream	**heúte**	today

A. CONSONANTS

1. *B* is generally pronounced like the English *b:*

Bett	bed
Gábe	gift

However, *b* at the end of a word is pronounced
like *p* in the English word "trap."

Grab	tomb
Trab	trot

2. *C* before *e, i, ä, ö, y* is pronounced like *ts:*
however, this is a rather rare combination. Generally *z* precedes these letters.
C before *a, o, u* is pronounced like *k*, but the
letter *k* is generally substituted. These two pro-
nunciations of the *c* occur mostly in foreign
words:

Cäsar	Caesar
Cato	Cato

3. *D* is generally pronounced like the English *d:*

Dátum	date
Nórden	Nord

However, *d* at the end of a word is pronounced
like *t* in the English word "but":

Bad	bath
Hund	dog

4. *F* is like the English *f*:

Flíege	fly
Fluss	river

5. *G* is generally pronounced as in the English
word "garden"; as in the English "general"
only in words of foreign origin:

Gárten	garden	**Garáge**	garage
Generál	general		

6. *H* is pronounced like the English *h* at the beginning of a word, or before an accented syllable.

húndert	hundred	**Geheímnis**	secret
Heímat	home		
	country	**behálten**	keep

In other cases, it is not pronounced:

Schuh	shoe	**frőhlich**	merry

7. *J* is pronounced like the English *y* as in "York":

Jahr	year
jemand	someone

8. *K* is pronounced like the English *c* before *a, o, u* ("canal," "corn," "cut"):

Kátze	cat	**Kéller**	cellar
Kind	child		

9. *L* is pronounced as in the English "land," "life," "loaf," never as in the English "wolf":

Land	land	**Lében**	life
Wolf	wolf		

LESSON 4

(Pronunciation Practice II)

10. *M* and *N* are pronounced as in English:

Meíle	mile
Máler	painter
nur	only
Néffe	nephew

11. *P* is also pronounced like the English *p:*

Preis	price
Pferd	horse

12. *Q*, always used in combination with *u*, is similar to the English *q:*

Quélle	spring
Qualitä́t	quality

13. *R* is more rolled than in English and always strongly pronounced, even at the end of a word:

Réde	speech
ínner	inside

14. *S* before a vowel is pronounced like the English *z* in "zoo":

süss	sweet
Sáhne	cream

At the end of a word or a syllable, it is pronounced as in the English "son":

Maus	mouse
Eis	ice

15. *T* is pronounced as in the English "tea":

Tanz	dance
Tásse	cup

There is no sound equivalent to the English *th.* This combination is simply pronounced like *t:*

Theater	theater
Thron	throne

16. *V* is pronounced, except in a few cases, like the English *f* in "fair":

Vogel	bird
Vater	father

The exceptions are a few Latin roots:

Vase	vase
Vulkan	volcano

17. *W* is pronounced like the English *v* in "vain," never like the English *w* in "want":

Wein	wine
Waffe	weapon

18. *X* is pronounced as in English:

Axt   axe
Hexe   witch

19. *Z* is pronounced like the English combination *ts:*

Zahn   tooth
Zauber   magic

B. SPECIAL GERMAN SOUNDS

Practice the following sounds which have as equivalents in English:

1. The German combination *ch* has three different sounds:

   a) the sound as pronounced in the English "character":

Christ   Christian
Chor   Chorus   **Charakter**   character

   When followed by an *s*, this combination has generally the sound of *ks:*

Fuchs   fox   **Wachs**   wax

   b) A sound near the English *h* in "hue":

China   China   *mich*   me
Kirche   church   *sicher*   certain

    c) A gutteral sound which does not exist in English but can be only approximated to the Scotch "loch":

Ach!	ah!	**Dach**	roof
Bach	brook	**Buch**	book

2. The suffix *ig* has a sound approximating *ch* except when followed by *lich* or *e;* in these cases, it is pronounced like *K:*

König	king	**Königlich**	kingly
ewig	eternal	**Ewigkeit**	eternity

3. Note the following combinations containing *s:*

    a) *sch,* equivalent to the English *sh* in "shoe":

Kirsche	cherry	**amerikanisch**	American
Schuh	shoe		

    b) *sp* or *st* at the beginning of a word, with the *s* sounded like *sh:*

stehen	(to) stand	**Spanien**	Spain
Stahl	steel	**Spiegel**	mirror

4. The combination *ng* is pronounced like the English *ng* in "sing"; the two letters are never pronounced separately:

bringen	(to) bring	**anfangen**	(to) begin

5. The combination *tz* is similar to the English *ts:*

Mütze	cap	**Blitz**	lightning

LESSON 5

(Alphabet)

3. THE GERMAN ALPHABET

Letter	Name	Letter	Name	Letter	Name
a	ah	i	ee	r	err
b	beh	j	yot	s	ess
c	tseh	k	kah	t	teh
d	deh	l	ell	u	oo
e	eh	m	em	v	fau
f	eff	n	en	w	veh
g	gay	o	oh	x	iks
h	hah	p	peh	y	üpsilonn
		q	ku	z	tsett

4. BUILDING A VOCABULARY

Building up a German vocabulary is a rather easy matter, since a great number of words are similar in German and English. Many words are spelled almost the same (though they may differ considerably in pronunciation).

Block	block	extra	extra
diagonal	diagonal	Drama	drama
Platz	place	Material	material
Land	land	Süden	South
Zentrum	center	Park	park
direkt	direct	Juwelen	jewels
Respekt	respect	Wolf	wolf
Frucht	fruit	Priester	priest
original	original	Kapelle	chapel
Problem	problem	Datum	date
Idee	idea	Intelligenz	intelligence
Leder	leather	Automobil	automobile
Hammer	hammer	Sekunde	second

Giraffe	giraffe	**Minúte**	minute
Appetít	appetite	**Konversatión**	conversation
Kapítel	chapter	**Instruktión**	instruction
Medizín	medicine	**Generál**	general
Nórden	North	**speziál**	special
Wésten	West	**Elemént**	element
Polizéi	police	**Präsidént**	president
Revolutión	revolution	**Akt**	act
Methóde	method	**modérn**	modern
blond	blonde	**Klásse**	class

LESSON 6

(General Equivalents)

GENERAL EQUIVALENTS

1. German *k*—English *c:*

Kanál	canal	*Respékt*	respect
Kolonie	colony	*Diréktor*	director

2. German *-ik*—English *-ic (s):*

Musík	music	*Politík*	politics
Physík	physics	*Lýrik*	lyrics

3. German *-ekt*—English *-ect:*

Effékt	effect	*Objékt*	object
Projékt	project	*Subjékt*	subject

4. German, *-heit, -keit, -tät*—English ending *-ty:*

Freíheit	liberty	*Schwíerigkeit*	difficulty
Schönheit	beauty	*Nótwendigkeit*	necessity
Autoritất	authority	*Qualitất*	quality

5. German *-enz*—English *-ncy:*

| *Frequénz* | frequency | *Tendénz* | tendency |

6. German *-ie*—English *-y:*

| *Geographíe* | geography | *Industríe* | industry |
| *Kopíe* | copy | *Philosophíe* | philosophy |

7. German *-tie*—English *-cy:*

| *Demokratíe* | democracy | *Diplomatíe* | diplomacy |

8. German *-ist*—English *-ist:*

| *Journalíst* | journalist | | |
| *Pianíst* | pianist | *Artíst* | artist |

9. German *sch*—English *sh:*

| *Schiff* | ship | *Wäsche* | washing |
| *Schuh* | shoe | *Schílling* | shilling |

10. German *-voll*—English *-ful:*

| *wúndervoll* | wonderful | *gedánkenvoll* | thoughtful |

11. German *-los*—English *-less:*

| *hérzlos* | heartless | *gerúchlos* | odorless |

12. German *-wärts*—English *-ward:*

| *wéstwärts* | westward | *vórwärts* | forward |

5. USEFUL WORD GROUPS

THE DAYS OF THE WEEK

Móntag	Monday
Dienstag	Tuesday
Míttwoch	Wednesday
Dónnerstag	Thursday
Freitag	Friday
Sámstag, or Sónnabend	Saturday
Sónntag	Sunday

THE MONTHS

Jánuar	January
Fébruar	February
März	March
Apríl	April
Mái	May
Júni	June
Júli	July
Augúst	August
Septémber	September
Október	October
Novémber	November
Dezémber	December

SOME NUMBERS

eins	one
zwei	two
drei	three
vier	four
fünf	five
sechs	six
sieben	seven
acht	eight
neun	nine
zehn	ten

SOME COLORS

blau	blue
rot	red
gelb	yellow
grün	green
weiss	white
schwarz	black
braun	brown
grau	gray

NORTH, SOUTH, EAST, WEST

Nórden	North
Súden	South
Ósten	East
Wésten	West

QUIZ 1

Try matching the following two columns:

1.	*Sonntag*	1.	Thursday
2.	*August*	2.	brown
3.	*Mittwoch*	3.	ten
4.	*grau*	4.	Sunday
5.	*Donnerstag*	5.	red
6.	*neun*	6.	August
7.	*braun*	7.	Monday
8.	*acht*	8.	July
9.	*Juli*	9.	five
10.	*gelb*	10.	white
11.	*rot*	11.	gray
12.	*Montag*	12.	nine
13.	*fünf*	13.	Wednesday
14.	*weiss*	14.	yellow
15.	*zehn*	15.	eight

ANSWERS

1—4; 2—6; 3—13; 4—11; 5—1; 6—12; 7—2; 8—15;
9—8; 10—14; 11—5; 12—7; 13—9; 14—10; 15—3.

WORD STUDY

The Word Studies point out words which are almost
similar in German and English.

Form	form	*Líste*	list
Post	mail	*Grúppe*	group
reich	rich	*Sórte*	sort
Súppe	soup	*Kapitän*	captain
Operatión	operation	*Admirál*	Admiral
Nóte	note	*Oránge*	orange
Diamánt	diamond	*Rátte*	rat
Pilót	pilot	*Camél*	camel
Pflánze	plant	*Pirát*	pirate
Sport	sport	*November*	November

LESSON 7

(Useful Phrases I)

6. GOOD MORNING!

Guten Morgen!	Hello! Good morning.
Herr	Mr.
Herr Wagner	Mr. Wagner
Guten Morgen, Herr Wagner.	Good morning, Mr. Wagner.
Guten Tag.	Good afternoon. (Good day.)
Guten Abend.	Good evening.
Frau	Mrs.
Frau Wagner	Mrs. Wagner
Guten Abend, Frau Wagner.	Good evening, Mrs. Wagner.
Gute Nacht.	Good night.

Gute Nacht, Frau Wagner.	Good night, Mrs. Wagner.
Wie geht es Ihnen?	How are you? How do you do? ("How is it going with you?")
Fräulein	Miss
Fräulein Wagner	Miss Wagner
Wie geht es Ihnen, Fräulein Wagner?	How do you do, Miss Wagner?
sehr	very
gut	well
Sehr gut.	Very well.
Danke.	Thank you. Thanks.
Danke schön	Thank you. ("Thank you nicely.")
Sehr gut, danke.	Very well, thanks.
Sprechen Sie.	Speak.
langsam	slowly
Sprechen Sie langsam.	Speak slowly.
bitte	please
Sprechen Sie langsam, bitte.	Speak slowly, please.
Wiederholen Sie.	Repeat.
Wiederholen Sie, bitte.	Please repeat.
danke	thanks
vielmals	much, a lot
Danke vielmals.	Thank you very much. Thanks a lot.
Keine Ursache.	Not at all. ("No reason.")
Ich danke Ihnen.	Thank you.
Ich danke Ihnen dafür.	Thank you for it.
Gern geschehen.	It was a pleasure. ("It happened with pleasure.")
Bis morgen.	Till tomorrow. See you tomorrow.

Bis Samstag.	Till Saturday. See you Saturday.
Bis Montag.	Till Monday. See you Monday.
Bis Donnerstag.	Till Thursday. See you Thursday.
Bis heute Abend.	Till this evening. See you this evening.
Bis morgen Abend.	Till tomorrow evening. See you tomorrow evening.
Bis nächste Woche.	Till next week. See you next week.
Bis später.	See you later.
Bis gleich.	See you in a little while.
Auf Wiedersehen.	Good-by.

QUIZ 2

1. sehr gut	1. speak
2. Guten Abend.	2. how
3. Sprechen Sie.	3. much, a lot
4. Danke.	4. See you tomorrow, (until tomorrow).
5. wie	5. How are you?
6. Bitte.	6. very well
7. viel	7. slowly
8. Bis morgen.	8. Thank you
9. Wie geht es Ihnen?	9. please
10. langsam	10. Good evening.

ANSWERS

1—6; 2—10; 3—1; 4—8; 5—2; 6—9; 7—3; 8—4; 9—5; 10—7.

LESSON 8

▱ ▱

(Useful Phrases II)

7. DO YOU HAVE . . . ?

Haben Sie . . . ?	Do you have . . . ?
Wasser	water
Zigaretten	some (any) cigarettes
Feuer	a light
Streichhölzer	some matches
Seife	some soap
etwas Papier	some paper

Notice that "a little" or "some" can be translated by *etwas*.

8. WHAT WILL YOU HAVE TO EAT?

das Frühstück	breakfast
das Mittagessen	lunch
das Abendessen	dinner, supper
Was wünschen Sie, mein Herr?	What will you have? ("What do you wish, sir?")
Guten Tag, mein Herr. Was wünschen Sie?	Good afternoon. What would you like? ("Good day, sir. What do you wish?")
Geben Sie mir . . .	Give me . . .
Geben Sie mir die Speisekarte.	Give me a menu. ("Let me have the menu.")
Ich möchte . . .	I'd like . . .
Brot	bread
Butter	butter
Suppe	soup
Fleisch	meat

Rindfleisch	beef
Eier	eggs
Gemüse	vegetables
Kartoffeln	potatoes
Salat	salad
Milch	milk
Wein	wine
Zucker	sugar
Salz	salt
Pfeffer	pepper
Bringen Sie mir . . .	Bring me . . .
einen Löffel	a spoon
einen Teelöffel	a teaspoon
eine Gabel	a fork
ein Messer	a knife
eine Serviette	a napkin
Einen Teller	a plate
ein Glas	a glass
Ich möchte . . .	I'd like . . .
ein Glas Wasser	a glass of water
eine Tasse Tee	a cup of tea
eine Tasse Kaffee	a cup of coffee
eine Flasche Wein	a bottle of wine
eine Flasche Weisswein	a bottle of white wine
eine Flasche Rotwein	a bottle of red wine
noch ein Ei	another egg
ein wenig davon	a little of that
noch ein wenig davon	a little more of that
noch etwas Brot, noch ein wenig Brot	some more bread, a little more bread
noch etwas Fleisch	some more meat
noch ein wenig Fleisch	a little more meat
die Rechnung, bitte	the check, please

QUIZ 3

1.	*Fleisch*	1.	Bring me . . .
2.	*Rotwein*	2.	matches
3.	*Haben Sie . . . ?*	3.	Give me . . .
4.	*Milch*	4.	meat
5.	*Butter*	5.	some water
6.	*Geben Sie mir . . .*	6.	a light
7.	*Streichhölzer*	7.	milk
8.	*noch etwas Brot*	8.	eggs
9.	*Bringen Sie mir . . .*	9.	red wine
10.	*Wasser*	10.	The check, please
11.	*Feuer*	11.	Do you have . . . ?
12.	*Salz*	12.	Butter
13.	*Eier*	13.	a cup of coffee
14.	*eine Tasse Kaffee*	14.	some more bread
15.	*Die Rechnung, bitte.*	15.	salt

ANSWERS

1—4; 2—9; 3—11; 4—7; 5—12; 6—3; 7—2; 8—14;
9—1; 10—5; 11—6; 12—15; 13—8; 14—13; 15—10.

LESSON 9

(Common Verb Forms)

9. COMMON VERB FORMS

In German there are two kinds of verbs:

     a. The weak (*schwache Zeitwörter*) or regular verbs.

     b. The strong (*starke Zeitwörter*) or irregular verbs.

1. I learn (weak)

ich lerne	I learn, I'm learning
du lernst	you (fam.) learn, you are learning
er (sie, es) lernt	he (she, it) learns, he is learning
wir lernen	we learn, we are learning
ihr lernt	you (fam.) learn, you are learning
Sie lernen	you (polite) learn, you are learning
sie lernen	they learn, they are learning

NOTES

a) Notice the endings:

ich	*-e*
du	*-st*
er (sie, es)	*-t*
wir	*-en*
ihr	*-t*
Sie, sie	*-en*

b) These forms, which make up the present tense, translate English "I learn," "I'm learning," and "I do learn."

c) *du lernst* and *ihr lernt*

The singular and the plural of these forms are used when you address one or several close friends. These *du* and *ihr* forms are called familiar forms. Notice the capital S in *Sie*. It is used to address one or several persons you don't know very well (whom you would not call by first name in English.) This *Sie* form is called the "polite" or formal form used either in direct speech or writing.

d) *Er lernt* means "he learns"; *sie lernt* means "she learns"; *es lernt* means "it learns"; *sie lernen* means "they learn" just as in English for all genders.

2. Learn! (Imperative)

Lerne!	Learn (the familiar form used to a person one knows well; compare *du lernst* above)
Lernt!	Learn (the familiar plural form; compare *ihr lernt* above)
Lernen Sie!	Learn! (the polite form; compare *Sie Lernen* above)
Lerne nicht!	Don't learn! (fam.)
Lernt nicht!	Don't learn! (fam. plural)
Lernen Sie nicht!	Don't lea.n! (polite)

This form of the verb which is used in commands and requests is called "the imperative."

3. I give (strong)

ich gebe	I give, I'm giving
du gibst	you (fam.) give, you're giving
er (sie, es) gibt	he (she, it) gives, he's giving
wir geben	we give, we're giving
ihr gebt	you (fam. plural) give, you're giving
Sie geben	you (polite) give, you're giving
sie geben	they give, they're giving
Gib!	Give! (fam.)
Gebt!	Give! (fam. plural)
Geben Sie!	Give! (polite)

Notice that in the case of the strong verb, the endings are the same as those of the weak verb, but the vowel of the stem changes in the second and third person singular.

4. I don't give

ich gebe	I give
ich gebe nicht	I don't give
ich gebe nicht	I don't give
du gibst nicht	you don't give
er (sie, es) gibt nicht	he (she, it) doesn't give
wir geben nicht	we don't give
ihr gebt nicht	you don't give
Sie geben nicht	you don't give
sie geben nicht	they don't give

10. ASKING A QUESTION

1. To ask a question you reverse the word order:

Sie lernen.	You learn. You're learning.
Lernen Sie?	Do you learn? Are you learning?
Lerne ich?	Do I learn?
Lernst du?	Do you learn?
Lernt er?	Does he learn?
Lernt sie?	Does she learn?
Lernen wir?	Do we learn?
Lernt ihr?	Do you learn?
Lernen Sie?	Do you learn?
Lernen sie?	Do they learn?

2. To ask a question in the negative form, also reverse the word order and use the negative *nicht*.

Lerne ich nicht?	Don't I learn?
Lernst du nicht?	Don't you learn?
Lernt er nicht?	Doesn't he learn?
Lernt sie nicht?	Doesn't she learn?
Lernen wir nicht?	Don't we learn?

Lernt ihr nicht?	Don't you learn?
Lernen Sie nicht?	Don't you learn?
Lernen sie nicht?	Don't they learn?

REVIEW QUIZ 1

Choose the correct German word equivalent to the English.

1. Five—
   a. *sechs*
   b. *seiben*
   c. *fünf*

2. Eight—
   a. *acht*
   b. *neun*
   c. *vier*

3. Tuesday—
   a. *Mittwoch*
   b. *Dienstag*
   c. *Freitag*

4. Sunday—
   a. *Sonntag*
   b. *Samstag*
   c. *Montag*

5. March—
   a. *März*
   b. *September*
   c. *April*

6. June—
   a. *Juli*
   b. *Juni*
   c. *Mai*

7. Red—
   a. *blau*
   b. *orange*
   c. *rot*

8. Green—
   a. *gelb*
   b. *grün*
   c. *grau*

9. Black—
   a. *schwarz*
   b. *braun*
   c. *weiss*

10. Brown—
    a. *schwarz*
    b. *rot*
    c. *braun*

11. Good Morning—
    a. *Guten Morgen*
    b. *Guten Abend*
    c. *wie*

12. Very well—
    a. *Danke*
    b. *sehr gut*
    c. *sehr*

CONVERSATIONAL GERMAN

27

13. Thank you—
   a. *gut*
   b. *danke*
   c. *sehr*

14. Please—
   a. *Sprechen Sie*
   b. *Danke*
   c. *Bitte*

15. Good-by—
   a. *Bis morgen*
   b. *Auf Wiedersehen*
   c. *Guten Tag*

16. He gives—
   a. *er gibt*
   b. *sie gibt*
   c. *sie geben*

17. We are learning—
   a. *wir lernen*
   b. *Sie geben*
   c. *wir geben*

18. I don't give—
   a. *er gibt nicht*
   b. *ich gebe*
   c. *ich gebe nicht*

19. Do you give?—
   a. *Geben Sie?*
   b. *Gibt er?*
   c. *Gibt sie?*

20. Do I give?—
   a. *Geben Sie?*
   b. *Gebe ich?*
   c. *Gibt er?*

ANSWERS

1—c; 2—a; 3—b; 4—a; 5—a; 6—b; 7—c; 8—b; 9—a; 10—c; 11—a; 12—b; 13—b; 14—c; 15—b; 16—a; 17—a; 18—c; 19—a; 20—b.

WORD STUDY

Anekdóte	anecdote
Patiént	patient
Film	film
Patriót	patriot
Dialékt	dialect
Detektív	detective
Talént	talent
Religión	religion
Líste	list
Experimént	experiment

LESSON 10

(Nouns, Adjectives)

11. THE GERMAN DECLENSION

In German, articles, nouns, adjectives, and pronouns undergo some changes in their endings. This variation is called "declension."

There are four cases:

1. The nominative case is used for the subject.

Das Buch ist hier.   The book is here.

2. The genitive case is used to denote possession, and after certain prepositions.

der Name des Lehrers (masc.)	the name of the teacher
die Farbe der Blume (fem.)	the color of the flower
während des Tages	during the day

3. The dative case is used for the indirect object or after certain prepositions.

der Mann mit dem Stock	the man with the stick
Der Fisch springt aus dem Wasser.	The fish jumps out of the water.
Er gibt dem Mädchen eine Puppe.	He gives the girl a doll.

4. The accusative case is used for the direct object and after certain prepositions.

Sie hält die Feder.	She is holding the pen.
Er geht durch den Wald.	He goes through the wood.

12. THE ARTICLE

In German there are three genders, masculine, feminine, and neuter. As already mentioned, the articles are declined in the four cases already given (No. 11).

1. The definite article is declined as follows:

	Masc.	Fem.	Neuter
Nom.	*der*	*die*	*das*
Gen.	*des*	*der*	*des*
Dat.	*dem*	*der*	*dem*
Acc.	*den*	*die*	*das*

Plural (all genders)

Nom.	*die*
Gen.	*der*
Dat.	*den*
Acc.	*die*

2. The indefinite article is declined as follows:

	Masc.	Fem.	Neuter
Nom.	*ein*	*eine*	*ein*
Gen.	*eines*	*einer*	*eines*
Dat.	*einem*	*einer*	*einem*
Acc.	*einen*	*eine*	*ein*

13. DECLENSION OF NOUNS

1. Note that the endings of nouns in the singular undergo no changes except for the addition of *s*

or *es* in the genitive singular of all neuter and most masculine nouns.

2. In the plural, an *n* should be added to the dative of all three genders. In previous usage an *e* was added to the masculine dative noun, but this tendency is falling into disuse.

PLURAL OF NOUNS

1. Masculine

   a) nominative plus *e*

der Abend — die Abende   evening

   b) nominative plus *er*

der Geist — die Geister   spirit

   c) nominative plus *e* and often ¨ (Umlaut) on the last vowel.

der Hut — die Hüte   hat
der Schub — die Schube   show

   d) nominative plus *er* and ¨ (Umlaut) on the last vowel.

der Mann — die Männer   man

   e) masculine nouns ending in *el, en, er* do not change their endings. A few have ¨ (Umlaut).

der Schlüssel — die Schlüssel   key
der Kuchen — die Kuchen   cake
der Maler — die Maler   artist
der Apfel — die Äpfel   apple
der Acker — die Äcker   field
der Ofen — die Öfen   oven

The plural of a certain number of masculine nouns, most of them ending in *e*, is formed in all their cases by the addition of an *n* or, if there is no *e*, by the addition of an *en*.

der Knabe	*— die Knaben*	boy
der Mensch	*— die Menschen*	person

2. Feminine

  a) Most feminine nouns form their plural by adding *n* or *en*.

die Tür	*— die Türen*	door
die Frage	*— die Fragen*	question
die Lampe	*— die Lampen*	lamp

  b) Some add *e* or *e* and ¨ (Umlaut) on the last vowel.

die Kenntnis	*— die Kenntnisse*	knowledge
die Frucht	*— die Früchte*	fruit

  c) Feminine words ending in *in* form their plural in *innen*.

die Schülerin	*— die Schülerinnen*	student

3. Neuter

  a) Some neuter nouns form their plural by adding -*er*.

das Bild	*die Bilder*	picture
das Licht	*die Lichter*	light
das Bad	*die Bäder*	bath

  b) some add an *e*.

das Heft	*die Hefte*	notebook

c) some add *en*.

das Auge	*die Augen*	eye
das Ohr	*die Ohren*	ear

d) Neuters ending in *en* do not vary.

das Mädchen	*die Mädchen*	girl

14. DECLENSION OF ADJECTIVES

1. a) The possessive adjectives and the word *kein* (not any) are declined like the indefinite article:

das Buch meines Bruders	my brother's book
Er hat keinen Hut.	He has no hat.

b) An adjective used predicatively is not declined:

Das Wasser ist warm.	The water is warm.

2. Adjectives may be declined in three ways:

    1. Without article or pronoun.
       In this case the adjective takes the same case ending as the definite article, except in the masculine and neuter genitive, where it takes *en* instead of *es:*

	Masc.	**Fem.**
Nom.	*rot**er** Wein*	*rot**e** Tinte*
Gen.	*rot**en** Weines*	*rot**er** Tinte*
Dat.	*rot**em** Wein*	*rot**er** Tinte*
Acc.	*rot**en** Wein*	*rot**e** Tinte*

	Neuter	**Plural (all genders)**
Nom.	*rot**es** Gold*	*rot**e** Weine*
Gen.	*rot**en** Goldes*	*rot**er** Weine*
Dat.	*rot**em** Gold*	*rot**en** Weinen*
Acc.	*rot**es** Gold*	*rot**e** Weine*

2. With the definite article the adjective takes an *e* in the following five cases:

Nominative singular: masculine, feminine and neuter.

Accusative singular: feminine and neuter.

en in all other cases.

	Masc.	**Fem.**
Nom.	*der rote Wein*	*die rote Tinte*
Gen.	*des roten Weines*	*der roten Tinte*
Dat.	*dem roten Wein*	*der roten Tinte*
Acc.	*den roten Wein*	*die rote Tinte*

	Neuter	**Plural (all genders)**
Nom.	*das rote Gold*	*die roten Weine*
Gen.	*des roten Goldes*	*der roten Weine*
Dat.	*dem roten Gold*	*den roten Weinen*
Acc.	*das rote Gold*	*die roten Weine*

3. Since the indefinite article has no ending in the masculine and neuter nominative and in the neuter accusative, in these cases the adjective takes the ending of the definite article. In the nominative and accusative feminine, it takes an *e;* in all other cases *en.*

	Masc.	**Fem.**
Nom.	*ein roter Wein*	*seine rote Tinte*
Gen.	*eines roten Weines*	*seiner roten Tinte*
Dat.	*einem roten Wein*	*seiner roten Tinte*
Acc.	*einen roten Wein*	*seine rote Tinte*

	Neuter	**Plural (all genders)**
Nom.	*kein rotes Gold*	*meine roten Weine*
Gen.	*keines roten Goldes*	*meiner roten Weine*
Dat.	*keinem roten Gold*	*meinen roten Weinen*
Acc.	*kein rotes Gold*	*meine roten Weine*

15. COMPARATIVE AND SUPERLATIVE

1. The comparative and the superlative are formed as in English by adding *er* for the comparative and *st* (or *est*) for the superlative to the adjective.

   Some short adjectives also take ¨ on their vowel.

schlecht, schlechter, schlechtest	bad, worse, worst
alt, älter, ältest	old, older, oldest

2. Than is translated by *als*.

3. The superlative is declined.

4. There are a few adjectives which have an irregular comparative. Here are the most common ones:

gut	*besser*	*der (die, das) beste*
	good, better, best	
gross	*grösser*	*der (die, das) grösste*
	big, bigger, biggest	
hoch	*höher*	*der (die, das) höchste*
	high, higher, highest	
nah	*näher*	*der (die, das) nächste*
	close, closer, closest	

5. Examples:

Das Mädchen ist kleiner als der Knabe.	The girl is smaller than the boy.
London ist die grösste Stadt in Europa.	London is the largest city in Europe.

16. PREPOSITIONS

The following prepositions always take the genitive:

während	during
wegen	because of
statt, anstatt	instead of
trotz	despite

während des Krieges	during the war
wegen der Leute	because of the people
anstatt einer Feder	instead of a pen
trotz der Kälte	despite the cold

The following always govern the accusative:

durch	through, by
für	for
gegen	against, toward
ohne	without
um	round, about, at (time)

durch die Stadt	through the city
für den Frieden	for the peace
gegen den Krieg	against the war
ohne einen Lehrer	without a teacher
um den See	around the lake

The following always govern the dative:

aus	from, out of
bei	at, by, near
mit	with
nach	after, to (place)
seit	since
von	of, by, from
zu	to, at

aus der Schule	out of the school
bei meinen Eltern	at my parents'
mit gutem Appetit	with a good appetite
nach dem Frühstück	after breakfast
seit einem Jahr	for (since) one year
von dem Hafen	from the port
zu den Bergen	to the mountains

The following take the accusative if they denote motion toward a place. In this case they are used in reply to the question, *"Wohin?"* (Where to?) But they also can take the dative if they denote rest (or motion) at a place. In this latter case they are used in reply to the question, *"Wo?"* (Where?)

an	at, to
auf	on, upon, in
hinter	behind
in	in, into, at
neben	beside, near
über	over, across
unter	under, among
vor	before, ago
zwischen	between

an der Ecke	at the corner
auf dem Land	in the country
hinter dem Hotel	behind the hotel
in dem Wasser	in the water
neben der Kirche	near the church
über den Wolken	over the clouds
unter dem Dach	under the roof
vor dem Rathaus	before the town hall
zwischen den Schultern	between the shoulders

Some of the above prepositions may be contracted with the definite article in the following way:

am	for	*an dem*
im	for	*in dem*
beim	for	*bei dem*
vom	for	*von dem*
zum	for	*zu dem*
zur	for	*zu der*
ins	for	*in das*

Examples:

Wo liegt Rom?	Where does Rome lie?
Rom liegt am Tiber.	Rome lies on the Tiber.
Wohin fahren Sie heute?	Where are you going today?
Ich fahre an den Strand.	I am going to the beach.
Wo steht die Lampe?	Where is the lamp standing?
Auf dem Tisch.	On the table.
Wohin gehen die Seeleute?	Where are the sailors going?
Sie gehen auf das Schiff.	They are going to the ship.
Wo liegt der Garten?	Where is the garden located?
Hinter dem Haus.	Behind the house.
Wohin stellen Sie den Schirm?	Where are you putting the umbrella?

Hinter die Tür.	Behind the door.
Wo wohnt Herr Müller?	Where does Mr. Müller live?
Er wohnt in dieser Strasse.	He lives in this street.
Wohin gehen die Leute?	Where are the people going?
Sie gehen ins Kino.	They are going to the movies.
Wo fliegt das Flugzeug?	Where is the plane flying?
Es fliegt über den Bergen.	It is flying over the mountains.
Wohin laufen die Kinder?	Where are the children running?
Sie laufen über die Brücke.	They are running over the bridge.
Wo ist die Katze?	Where is the cat?
Unter dem Bett.	Under the bed.
Wohin legt er das Heft?	Where is he putting the notebook?
Er legt es unter das Lineal.	He is putting it under the ruler.
Wo ist der Brunnen?	Where is the fountain?
Vor dem Tor.	In front of the gate.
Wohin tragen Sie den Koffer?	Where are you carrying the suitcase?
Vor das Zollamt.	In front of the customs house.
Wo liegt Luxemburg?	Where is Luxemburg located?
Es liegt zwischen Deutschland und Frankreich.	It is located between Germany and France.
Wohin legen Sie den Bleistift?	Where are you putting the pencil?
Zwischen die Seiten des Buches.	Between the pages of the book.

LESSON 11

(Asking Your Way)

17. ASKING YOUR WAY

1. Where?

Verzeihung, mein Herr.	Excuse me, Sir.
wo	where
ist,	is
Wo ist es?	Where is it?
das Hotel	the hotel
Wo ist das Hotel?	Where is the hotel?
Wo ist das Restaurant?	Where is the restaurant?
Wo ist das Telefon?	Where is the telephone?
Können Sie mir sagen . . . ?	Can you tell me . . . ?
Können Sie mir sagen, wo das Telefon ist?	Can you tell me where the telephone is?
Können Sie mir sagen, wo der Bahnhof ist?	Can you tell me where the (railroad) station is?

2. Here and There.

hier	here
dort	there
dort drüben	over there
Welche Richtung ist es?	Which way is it?
hier entlang	this way
dort entlang	that way
hier hinunter	over this way

dort hinunter	over that way
Das ist dort entlang.	It's over that way.
rechts	to the right
links	to the left
rechts von Ihnen	to your right
zu Ihrer linken	to your left
auf der linken Seite	on your left
Das ist rechts.	It's to the right.
Das ist links.	It's to the left.
Beigen Sie rechts ein.	Turn right.
Biegen Sie links ein.	Turn left.
Gehen Sie geradeaus.	Keep straight on.
Das ist geradeaus.	It's straight ahead.
Das ist geradeaus vor Ihnen.	It's straight ahead of you.
Gehen Sie geradeaus.	Go straight ahead.
Es ist direkt gegenüber.	It's directly opposite.
Es ist weiter oben.	It's above.
Es ist weiter unten.	It's below.
Es ist auf der Ecke.	It's on the corner.
Es ist nicht hier.	It's not here.
Es ist nicht dort.	It's not there.
Es ist hier.	It's here.
Es ist nicht hier.	It's not here.
Es ist dort.	It's there.
Es ist dort drüben.	It's over there.
Es ist dort oben.	It's up there.
Er ist hier.	He's here.
Kommen Sie her.	Come here.
Bleiben Sie hier.	Stay here.
Warten Sie dort.	Wait there.
Gehen Sie hier entlang.	Go this way.

Gehen Sie dort entlang.	Go that way.
Wer ist dort?	Who's there?
Legen Sie es hierhin.	Put it here.
Legen Sie es dorthin.	Put it there.

LESSON 12

(Near, Far, There, To Be)

3. Near and Far.

nah	near
nah bei	near here
sehr na he	very near; quite close
in der Nähe des Dorfes	near the village
in der Nähe der Strasse	near the road
in seiner Nähe	near him
Es ist sehr nah.	It's very near.
Es ist ganz in der Nähe.	It's very near here.
weit	far
Ist es weit?	Is it far?
Es ist weit.	It's far.
Es ist nicht weit.	It's not far.
Das ist weit von hier.	That's far from here.

4. There.

dort, da	there
Ist er in Paris?	Is he in Paris?
Ja, er ist dort.	Yes, he is (there).
Ist Paul da?	Is Paul there?
Ja, er ist da.	Yes, he's there
Geht er nach Frankfurt?	Is he going to Frankfort?

Ja, er geht dorthin.	Yes, he's going there.
Ich gehe dorthin.	I'm going there.
Ich will nicht dorthin fahren.	I don't want to go there.
Ich wohen dort.	I live there.

QUIZ 4

1. *Können Sie mir sagen, wo das Telefon ist?*	1. It's this way.
2. *Wo befindet sich das Hotel?*	2. It's to the right.
3. *Das ist hier entlang.*	3. Turn left.
4. *Das ist rechts geradeaus.*	4. That's (directly) opposite.
5. *Das ist zur rechten.*	5. It's straight ahead.
6. *Er wohnt dort.*	6. Can you tell me where the telephone is?
7. *Warten Sie dort.*	7. Where is the hotel? ("Where does the hotel find itself?")
8. *Gehen Sie hier entlang.*	8. He lives there.
9. *Biegen Sie links ein.*	9. That's not here.
10. *Das ist gegenüber.*	10. Stay here.
11. *Das ist nicht weit.*	11. Wait there.
12. *Legen Sie es dorthin.*	12. Go this way.
13. *Das ist nicht hier.*	13. Who's there?
14. *Bleiben Sie hier.*	14. Put it there.
15. *Wer ist dort?*	15. It's not far.

ANSWERS

1—6; 2—7; 3—1; 4—5; 5—2; 6—8; 7—11; 8—12; 9—3; 10—4; 11—15; 12—14; 13—9; 14—10; 15—13.

WORD STUDY

Instruktión (die)	instruction
energisch	energetic
Instrumént (das)	instrument
Regimént (das)	regiment
Violíne (die)	violin
Palást (der)	palace
Terrásse (die)	terrace
nationál	national
Sardíne (die)	sardine
Skandál (der)	scandal

18. TO BE OR NOT TO BE

TO BE

1. I am, you are, he is

ich bin	I am
du bist	you are
er ist	he is
sie ist	she is
es ist	it is
wir sind	we are
ihr seid	you are
Sie sind	you are
sie sind	they are

NOT TO BE

2. I am not, you are not

ich bin nicht	I am not
du bist nicht	you are not
er ist nicht	he is not
sie ist nicht	she is not
es ist nicht	it is not
wir sind nicht	we are not

ihr seid nicht	you are not
Sie sind nicht	you are not
sie sind nicht	they are not

Seien Sie!	Be!
Seien Sie ruhig.	Be quiet. Don't worry.
Ich bin Amerikaner.	I'm (an) American.
Ich bin im Zimmer.	I'm in the room.
Ich bin im Hotel.	I'm at the hotel.
Er ist hier.	He's here.
Sie ist dort.	She's there.
Sie sind hier.	They're here.
Sie sind dort drüben.	They're over there.

Ich bin bereit.	I'm ready.
Sie ist bereit.	She's ready.
Sie sind bereit.	They're ready.

Sind Sie sicher, mein Herr?	Are you certain, sir?
Sind Sie sicher, meine Dame?	Are you certain, madam?
Sind Sie sicher, mein Fräulein?	Are you certain, miss?
Sind Sie sicher, meine Herren?	Are you certain, gentlemen?
Sind Sie sicher, meine Damen?	Are you certain, ladies?

Sind Sie Engländer?	Are you English?
Ja, ich bin Engländer.	Yes, I'm English.
Nein, ich bin nicht Engländer.	No, I'm not English.
Wie spät ist es?	What time is it?
Wo sind Sie her?	Where are you from?
Ich bin aus Berlin.	I'm from Berlin.

3. Am I? Are you?

Bin ich?	Am I?
Bist du?	Are you?
Ist er?	Is he?
Ist sie?	Is she?
Ist es?	Is it?
Sind wir?	Are we?
Seid ihr?	Are you?
Sind Sie?	Are you?
Sind sie	Are they?

4. Where am I?

Wo bin ich?	Where am I?
Wo bist du?	Where are you?
Wo ist er?	Where is he?
Wo ist sie?	Where is she?
Wo ist es?	Where is it?
Wo sind wir?	Where are we?
Wo seid ihr?	Where are you?
Wo sind Sie?	Where are you?
Wo sind sie?	Where are they?

19. MY, YOUR, HIS, HER

*The possessive adjectives are declined like the article
ein.*

Wo ist mein Buch?	Where is my book?
Wo ist dein Buch?	Where is your (familiar) book?
Wo ist sein Buch?	Where is his book?
Wo ist ihr Buch?	Where is her book?
Wo ist Ihr Buch?	Where is your (polite, sing.) book?

Wo ist unser Buch?	Where is our book?
Wo ist euer Buch?	Where is your (familiar) book?
Wo ist Ihr Buch?	Where is your (polite, pl.) book?
Wo ist ihr Buch?	Where is their book?
Wo ist meine Feder?	Where is my pen?
Wo ist deine Feder?	Where is your (familiar) pen?
Wo ist seine Feder?	Where is his pen?
Wo ist ihre Feder?	Where is her pen?
Wo is Ihre Feder?	Where is your (polite, sing.) pen?
Wo ist unsere Feder?	Where is our pen?
Wo ist eure Feder?	Where is your (familiar) pen?
Wo ist Ihre Feder?	Where is your (polite, pl.) pen?
Wo ist ihre Feder?	Where is their pen?
Wo sind meine Bücher?	Where are my books?
Wo sind deine Bücher?	Where are your (familiar) books?
Wo sind seine Bücher?	Where are his books?
Wo sind ihre Bücher?	Where are her books?
Wo sind Ihre Bücher?	Where are your (polite, sing.) books?
Wo sind unsere Bücher?	Where are our books?
Wo sind eure Bücher?	Where are your (familiar) books?
Wo sind Ihre Bücher?	Where are your (polite, pl.) books?
Wo sind ihre Bücher?	Where are their books?

(Note that the endings of the plural of the personal pronouns remain the same regardless of the gender of the noun)

Wo sind meine Federn?	Where are my pens?
Wo sind deine Federn?	Where are your (familiar) pens?
Wo sind seine Federn?	Where are his pens?
Wo sind Ihre Federn?	Where are your (polite, sing.) pens?
Wo sind ihre Federn?	Where are her pens?
Wo sind unsere Federn?	Where are our pens?
Wo sind eure Federn?	Where are your (familiar) pens?
Wo sind Ihre Federn?	Where are your (polite, pl.) pens?
Wo sind ihre Federn?	Where are their pens?

QUIZ 5

1.	*Wo sind Sie her?*	1.	What time is it?
2.	*Wie spät ist es?*	2.	Where are you from?
3.	*Er ist hier.*	3.	Where is he?
4.	*Ich bin bereit.*	4.	Where is her letter?
5.	*Sind Sie sicher?*	5.	They are ready.
6.	*Wo ist er?*	6.	Where are their books?
7.	*Wo ist ihr Brief?*	7.	I'm ready.
8.	*Wo sind ihre Bücher?*	8.	I'm at the hotel.
9.	*Sie sind bereit.*	9.	Are you certain?
10.	*Seien Sie ruhig.*	10.	He's here.
11.	*Ich bin im Hotel.*	11.	I'm (an) American.
12.	*Ich bin Amerikaner.*	12.	Don't worry.
13.	*Ich bin nicht bereit.*	13.	I'm from Berlin.
14.	*Wir sind hier.*	14.	I'm not ready.
15.	*Ich bin aus Berlin.*	15.	We are here.

ANSWERS

1—2; 2—1; 3—10; 4—7; 5—9; 6—3; 7—4; 8—6;
9—5; 10—12; 11—8; 12—11; 13—14; 14—15;
15—13.

LESSON 13

(It Is, Questions)

20. IT IS, THAT IS.
ES IST, DAS IST.

Es ist gut.	It's good.
Das ist gut.	That's good.
Das ist nicht gut.	It's not good.
Das ist in Ordnung.	It's (that's) all right. (It's in order.)
Das ist nicht in Ordnung.	It's not very good (nice). It's not right (fair).
Das ist schlecht.	It's bad.
Das ist nicht schlecht.	It's not bad.
Das ist klein.	It's small.
Das ist gross.	It's big.
Das ist nichts.	It's nothing.
Das ist schwer.	It's hard (difficult).
Das ist leicht.	It's easy.
Das ist sehr leicht.	It's very easy.
Das ist leicht genug.	It's easy enough.
Das ist leichter.	It's easier.
Das ist weniger schwer.	It's less difficult.
Das ist weit.	It's far.
Das ist nicht sehr weit.	It's not very far.
Das ist in der Nähe.	It's near here.
Das ist sehr in der Nähe.	It's very near here.

Das ist wenig.	It's (a) little.
Das ist zu wenig.	It's too little.
Das ist genug.	It's enough.
Das ist viel.	It's a lot.
Das ist dort.	It's there.
Das ist dort drüben.	It's over there.
Das ist nicht dort.	It's not there.
Das ist hier.	It's here.
Das ist nicht hier.	It's not here.
Das ist hier entlang.	It's this way.
Das ist dort entlang.	It's that way.
Das ist für mich.	It's for me.
Das ist für dich.	It's for you (fam.).
Das ist für ihn.	It's for him.
Das ist für sie.	It's for her.
Das ist für Sie.	It's for you (polite, sing. and pl.).
Das ist für uns.	It's for us.
Das ist für euch.	It's for you (fam. pl.).
Das ist für sie.	It's for them.
Das ist nicht für sie.	It's not for them.
Das ist für die Kinder.	It's for the children.
Das ist es.	That's it.
Das ist das.	That's it. (That's right.)

21. ASKING A QUESTION

1. Reverse the order.
2. Regular word order with the question intonation (that is, with the pitch of the voice raised at the end of the sentence).

Ist es das?	Is it that? Is it this?
Das ist es?	That is it?
Er ist hier. (statement)	He's here.
Er ist hier? (question)	Is he here?
Das ist wahr. (state.)	It's true.
Das ist wahr? (quest.)	Is it true?

Wo ist er?	Where is he?
Wo ist es?	Where is it?
Ist er bereit?	Is he ready?
Sind Sie bereit?	Are you ready?
Sind sie bereit?	Are they ready?
Kommen Sie?	Are you coming?
Haben Sie Zigaretten?	Do you have any cigarettes?
Haben Sie Feuer?	Do you have a light?
Sprechen Sie Englisch?	Do you speak English?
Sprechen Sie Deutsch?	Do you speak German?

WORDS

Ásien (das)	Asia
alt	old
Feld (das)	field
Álpen (die)	Alps
Augúst (der)	August
Lektión (die)	lesson
Náse (die)	nose
Bär (der)	bear
Tíger (der)	tiger
Elefánt (der)	elephant

LESSON 14

(To Have)

22. TO HAVE AND HAVE NOT

haben	to have

1. I have

ich habe	I have
du hast	you have
er hat	he has

wir haben	we have
ihr habt	you have
Sie haben	you have
sie haben	they have

2. I don't have

ich habe nicht	I don't have, I haven't
du hast nicht	you don't have, etc.
er hat nicht	he doesn't have
wir haben nicht	we don't have
ihr habt nicht	you don't have
Sie haben nicht	you don't have
sie haben nicht	they don't have
Ich habe etwas.	I have something. I've got something.
Ich habe nichts.	I have nothing. I don't have anything. There's nothing wrong with me.
Ich habe Geld.	I have money.
Ich habe genug Geld.	I have enough money.
Ich habe kein Geld.	I have no money. I haven't any money.
Ich habe genug Zeit.	I have enough time.
Sie haben keine Zigaretten.	They don't have any cigarettes.
Ich habe Hunger.	I'm hungry.
Er hat Hunger.	He's hungry.
Ich habe Durst.	I'm thirsty.
Er hat recht.	He's right.
Er hat unrecht.	He's wrong.
Sie haben recht.	You're right.
Sie hat Angst.	She's afraid.
Ich habe Zahnschmerzen.	I have a toothache.
Sie hat Kopfschmerzen.	She has a headache.

3. Do I have?

habe ich?	do I have?
hast du?	do you have?
hat er?	does he have?
haben wir?	do we have?
habt ihr?	do you have?
haben Sie?	do you have (polite)?
haben sie?	do they have?

4. Don't I have?

habe ich nicht?	don't I have? haven't I?
hast du nicht?	don't you have?
hat er hicht?	doesn't he have?
haben wir nicht?	don't we have?
habt ihr nicht?	don't you have?
haben Sie nicht?	don't you have?
haben sie nicht?	don't they have?

Hat er Geld?	Does he have any money?
Hat sie genug Geld?	Does she have enough money?
Hat er Freunde in Berlin?	Does he have (any) friends in Berlin?
Haben Sie einen Bleistift?	Do you have a pencil?
Haben Sie eine Feder?	Do you have a pen?
Haben Sie eine Briefmarke?	Do you have a stamp?
Haben Sie etwas Papier?	Do you have any paper?
Haben Sie Zigaretten?	Do you have any cigarettes?
Haben Sie Feuer?	Do you have a light?
Haben Sie ein Streichholz?	Do you have a match?
Was haben Sie?	What's the matter with you? What hurts you?

Was hat er?	What's the matter with him?
Haben Sie Zeit mit mir zu sprechen?	Do you have time to talk to me?

LESSON 15

(Words and Idioms)

23. SOME WORDS AND IDIOMS

1. There is

Es gibt . . .	There is . . .
Es gibt etwas.	There is something.
Es gibt nichts.	There is nothing.
Es gibt nichts mehr.	There isn't any more.
Es gibt nichts mehr davon.	There isn't any more of that.
Keine Antwort.	No answer.
Es gibt keinen Unterschied.	There's no difference.
Es gibt keine Schwierigkeit.	There's no difficulty.
Niemand ist dort.	No one is there.
Niemand ist hier.	No one is here.
Sind Briefe für mich da?	Are there any letters for me?
Ist Post da?	Is there any mail?
Ist Post für mich da?	Is there any mail for me?
Sind viele Menschen da?	Are there many people?
Gibt es ein Telefon hier?	Is there a telephone here?
Gibt es ein Restaurant in der Nähe?	Is there a restaurant nearby?

Ist eine Apotheke in der Nähe?	Is there a druggist nearby?
Gibt es ein Café in der Nähe?	Is there a café nearby?
Hier sind vier Personen.	There are four people here.

2. ago

vor	ago
vor einer Stunde	an hour ago
vor zwei Stunden	two hours ago
vor drei Stunden	three hours ago
vor einem Tag	a day ago
vor zwei Tagen	two days ago
vor drei Wochen	three weeks ago
vor fünf Monaten	five months ago
vor fünf Jahren	five years ago
vor zehn Jahren	ten years ago
vor langer Zeit	a long time ago
vor ziemlich langer Zeit	a pretty long time ago
vor nicht langer Zeit	not so long ago
vor kurzer Zeit	a short time ago

3. also

auch	also, too
ich auch	I also (too)
du auch	you also (too)
er auch	he also
sie auch	she also (too)
wir auch	we also (too)
ihr auch	you also (too)
Sie auch	you also (too)
sie auch	they also (too)

Er kommt auch.	He's coming too.
Sie kommen auch.	They're coming, too.
Er hat es auch getan.	He did it too.
Ich komme auch.	I'm coming, too.
Sie sind so gross wie die andern.	They're as tall as the others.
Sie sind nicht so klein wie die andern.	They're not as small as the others.
Das ist nicht so gut wie das andere.	That's not as good as the other.
Das ist nicht so gross wie das andere.	That's not as large as the other.
Kommen Sie so schnell wie möglich.	Come as quickly as you can.
Tun Sie es so schnell wie möglich.	Do it as soon as possible.
Machen Sie es so gut wie möglich.	Do it as well as possible.

QUIZ 6

1.	Ich habe genug Zeit.	1.	Not at all. Don't mention it.
2.	Er hat recht.	2.	There's no answer.
3.	Ich brauche das.	3.	There's no difference.
4.	Er hat unrecht.	4.	There's no difficulty.
5.	Ihm ist kalt.	5.	Are there any letters for me?
6.	Ich habe Hunger.	6.	There's nobody here.
7.	Ich bin zwanzig Jahre alt.	7.	A day ago.
8.	Ich habe Durst.	8.	Three weeks ago.
9.	Wie alt sind Sie?	9.	A long time ago.
10.	Hat er Geld?	10.	Come as quickly as you can.

11. *Wieviel haben Sie davon?*	11. I have nothing. I don't have anything. There's nothing wrong with me.
12. *Hat er Freunde in Paris?*	12. I have enough time.
13. *Ich habe nichts.*	13. I'm hungry.
14. *Sie haben recht.*	14. I'm thirsty.
15. *Was hat er?*	15. He's cold.
16. *Seit drei Wochen.*	16. He's right.
17. *Es gibt keinen Unterschied.*	17. He's wrong.
18. *Es gibt keine Schwierigkeit.*	18. You're right.
19. *Keine Ursache.*	19. I need that.
20. *Seit langer Zeit.*	20. I'm twenty (years old).
21. *Niemand ist hier.*	21. Does he have (any) money?
22. *Kommen Sie so schnell wie möglich.*	22. Does he have (any) friends in Paris?
23. *Sind Briefe für mich da?*	23. What's the matter with him?
24. *Seit einem Tag.*	24. How old are you?
25. *Keine Antwort.*	25. How many of them do you have?

ANSWERS

1—12; 2—16; 3—19; 4—17; 5—15; 6—13; 7—20; 8—14; 9—24; 10—21; 11—25; 12—22; 13—11; 14—18; 15—23; 16—8; 17—3; 18—4; 19—1; 20—9; 21—6; 22—10; 23—5; 24—7; 25—2.

LESSON 16

(Phrases I)

24. DO YOU SPEAK GERMAN?

Sprechen Sie Deutsch?	Do you speak German?
Nein, Ich spreche nicht Deutsch.	No, I don't speak German.
Ich spreche nicht gut Deutsch.	I don't speak German very well.
schlecht	poorly
sehr schlecht	very poorly
Ich spreche sehr schlecht.	I speak very poorly.
ein wenig	a little
Ja, ich spreche ein wenig.	Yes, I speak a little.
sehr wenig	very little
Ich spreche sehr wenig.	I speak very little.
Ein paar Wörter.	A few words.
Nur ein paar Wörter.	Only a few words.
Verstehen Sie?	Do you understand?
Nein, ich verstehe nicht.	No, I don't understand.
Ich verstehe nicht sehr gut.	I don't understand very well.
Ich verstehe Deutsch nicht sehr gut.	I don't understand German very well.
Ja, ich verstehe.	Yes, I understand.
Ja, ich verstehe ein wenig.	Yes, I understand a little.
Ich lese, aber ich kann nicht sprechen.	I read but I can't speak.
Verstehen Sie?	Do you understand?
Überhaupt nicht.	Not at all.

Schreiben Sie es.	Write it (down).
Wie schreiben Sie es?	How do you write (spell) it?
Ich kenne das Wort nicht.	I don't know that word.

25. PLEASE SPEAK A LITTLE SLOWER

Wenn Sie langsam sprechen, kann ich Sie verstehen.

If you speak slowly, I can understand you, or, If you speak slowly, I'll be able to understand you.

LESSON 17

(Phrases II, This, That)

Was haben Sie gesagt?	What did you say? You were saying? What was that?
Wie bitte, was haben Sie gesagt?	What did you say? ("How, please, what did you say?")
Wie sagen Sie das auf deutsch?	How do you say that in German?
Wie sagt man "Thank you" auf deutsch?	How do you say "Thank you" in German?
Was wollen Sie sagen?	What do you want to say?
würden Sie	would you . . . ?
sprechen	(to) speak
etwas langsamer	more slowly ("somewhat slower")
Würden Sie etwas langsamer sprechen?	Would you speak more slowly?

bitte	please
Würden Sie bitte etwas langsamer sprechen?	Would you mind speaking a little more slowly, please?
ich bitte Sie	please ("I beg you")
Ich bitte Sie etwas langsamer zu sprechen.	Would you mind speaking a little more slowly, please?
Würden Sie das bitte wiederholen?	Would you please say that again? ("Would you repeat that, please?")

26. THANKS

Bitte, sprechen Sie langsam.	Please speak slowly.
Danke.	Thanks.
Ich danke Ihnen.	Thanks. ("I thank you.")
Ich danke Ihnen vielmals.	Thank you very much.
Keine Ursache.	Don't mention it. ("no cause")
Danke schön.	Thanks. ("Thank you nicely.")
Bitte schön.	Not at all.
Entschuldigen Sie, bitte.	Excuse me.
Bitte sehr.	Certainly.
Gestatten Sie?	May I? ("You permit me?")
Bitte sehr!	Of course! Please do!
Ich bitte Sie.	Please do! ("I beg you.")

Wie bitte?	Pardon? What did you say?
Verzeihung, was sagen Sie?	Sorry. What are you saying?
Auf Wiedersehen!	Good-by. See you soon.
Auf baldiges Wiedersehen!	See you soon. See you later.
Bis heute Abend.	See you this evening. ("Until this evening.")

QUIZ 7

1. Schreiben Sie.	1. No, I don't speak German.
2. Nein, ich spreche nicht Deutsch.	2. A few words.
3. Ich verstehe Deutsch nicht gut.	3. Do you understand?
4. Verstehen Sie?	4. I don't understand German very well.
5. Ein paar Wörter.	5. Write!
6. Wollen Sie das bitte wiederholen?	6. How do you write (spell) it?
7. Wie sagt man "Thank you" auf deutsch?	7. I don't know that word.
8. Was wollen Sie sagen?	8. How do you say "Thank you" in German?
9. Wie schreiben Sie es?	9. What do you mean? ("What do you want to say?")
10. Ich kenne das Wort nicht.	10. Would you please repeat that?

ANSWERS

1—5; 2—1; 3—4; 4—3; 5—2; 6—10; 7—8; 8—9; 9—6; 10—7.

WORD STUDY

Äquátor (der)	equator
backen	(to) bake
Ballón (der)	balloon
Gras (das)	grass
Problém (das)	problem
weíse	wise
Arm (der)	arm
Hónig (der)	honey
Wínter (der)	winter
Sómmer (der)	summer

27. THIS AND THAT

Dieser, diese, dieses follow the same declension as *der, die, das*

dieser Morgen	this or that morning
diese Nacht	this night
dieses Wochenende	this weekend
dieser Mann	this man
diese Frau	this woman
dieses Kind	this child

To express "that one" in contrast with "this," German simply uses *der (die, das)* with a special emphasis in the pronunciation.

Dieser Tisch ist breit und **der** *ist schmal.*
This table is wide and that one is narrow.

Diese Wand ist dick und **die** *ist dünn.*
This wall is thick and that one is thin.

Dieses Kleid ist lang und **das** *ist kurz.*
This dress is long and that one is short.

Dieser and *der* are interchangeable, so that you could also say:

Der *Tisch ist breit und dieser ist schmal.*
Dieser Hund ist gross und **der** *is klein.*
Diese Katze ist grau und **die** *ist schwarz.*
Das Bild ist gut und **dieses** *ist schlecht.*

Note that both *dieser* and *der* can mean either "this" or "that," although the basic meaning of *dieser* is "this."

QUIZ 8

1. *Ich bevorzuge diesen.*
2. *Was bedeutet das?*
3. *Geben Sie mir das.*
4. *Dieses gehört mir und das gehört Ihnen.*
5. *Das hängt davon ab.*
6. *Das ist es nicht.*
7. *Wie geht's?*
8. *Das ist selbstverständlich.*
9. *Das ist mir gleich.*
10. *Dieses gehört mir.*

1. What does this mean?
2. This is mine.
3. That goes without saying.
4. It's not that.
5. This one is mine and that one is yours.
6. Give me that.
7. It's all the same to me.
8. That depends.
9. How are you?
10. I prefer that one (masc.).

ANSWERS

1—10; 2—1; 3—6; 4—5; 5—8; 6—4; 7—9; 8—3;
9—7; 10—2.

WORD STUDY

Sympatíe (die)	sympathy
illustríeren	illustrate
Gymnástik (die)	gymnastics
Kristáll (das)	crystal
fríeren	(to) freeze
pácken	(to) pack
Gott (der)	God
Brust (die)	breast
Pomáde (die)	pomade
Lokomotíve (die)	locomotive

LESSON 18

(Not)

28. NOT

Das ist nicht gut.	That's not good.
Es ist nicht schlecht.	It's not bad.
Das ist es nicht.	That's not it.
Es ist nicht hier.	It's not here.
Nicht zuviel.	Not too much.
Nicht zu schnell.	Not too fast.
Nicht viel.	Not much.
Nicht viele.	Not many.
Nicht genug.	Not enough.
Nicht oft.	Not often.
Noch nicht.	Not yet.
Überhaupt nicht.	Not at all.

Ich habe keine Zeit.	I haven't any time.
	I have no time.
Ich weiss nicht wie.	I don't know how.
Ich weiss nicht wo.	I don't know where.
Ich weiss überhaupt nichts.	I don't know anything.
	I know nothing at all.
Er hat nichts gesagt.	He didn't say (hasn't said) anything.

29. NOTHING, NEVER, ETC.

Nichts.	Nothing.
Ich habe nichts.	I haven't anything.
Niemals, nie.	Never.
Ich sehe ihn nie.	I never see him.
Er kommt nie.	He never comes.
Wer ist gekommen?— Niemand.	Who came?—Nobody.
Ich sehe niemand.	I don't see anyone.
Ich gehe nicht mehr dorthin.	I don't go there any more.
Er kommt nicht mehr.	He doesn't come any more.
Ich habe nur hundert Mark.	I have only a hundred marks.
Du hast nur eine Stunde.	You have only one hour.
Er hat nur zehn davon.	He has only ten of them.

Declension of the personal pronoun.

Singular

Nom:	*ich*	*du*	*er*	*sie*	*es*
Dat:	*mir*	*dir*	*ihm*	*ihr*	*ihm*
Acc:	*mich*	*dich*	*ihn*	*sie*	*se*

Plural

Nom:	*wir*	*ihr*	*Sie*	*sie*
Dat:	*uns*	*euch*	*Ihnen*	*ihnen*
Acc:	*uns*	*euch*	*Sie*	*sie*

Examples:

Ich gebe dir ein Buch.	I give you a book.
Er spricht mit mir.	He is speaking to me.
Sie liebt mich.	She loves me.
Du sprichst mit ihm.	You are speaking with him.
Er hat dich gern.	He likes you.
Wir geben ihr Blumen.	We are giving her flowers.
Wir haben sie gesprochen.	We have spoken to her.
Ihr habt es ihm gegeben.	You have given it to him.
Er gibt Ihnen eine Feder.	He is giving you (polite) a pen.
Sie haben ihnen Geld gegeben.	They have given you money.
Ich habe euch etwas gegeben.	I have given you something.
Er hat uns nicht sprechen lassen.	He did not let us speak.

30. ISN'T IT?

Nicht wahr?	Isn't it?
Das ist schön, nicht wahr?	It's nice, isn't it?
Sie kommen, nicht wahr?	You're coming, aren't you?
Sie haben genug davon, nicht wahr?	You have enough of it, haven't you?
Sie haben keine, nicht wahr?	You haven't any, have you?

Sie sind einverstanden, nicht wahr?

You agree, don't you?

QUIZ 9

1. *Das ist es nicht.*	1. I don't see anyone.
2. *Ich weiss nicht wann.*	2. I have only a hundred marks.
3. *Ich habe keine Zeit.*	3. You have only one hour.
4. *Nichts.*	4. You're coming, aren't you?
5. *Sie kommen, nicht wahr?*	5. You haven't any of it, have you?
6. *Sie haben nur eine Stunde.*	6. That's not it.
7. *Ich sehe niemand.*	7. I haven't any time. I have no time.
8. *Ich habe nur hundert Mark.*	8. I don't know when.
9. *Sie haben keine davon, nicht wahr?*	9. He didn't say (hasn't said) anything.
10. *Er hat nichts gesagt.*	10. Nothing.

ANSWERS

1—6; 2—8; 3—7; 4—10; 5—4; 6—3; 7—1; 8—2; 9—5; 10—9.

31. I, YOU, HIM

1. It's me (I).

Ich bin es.	It's me (I).
Du bist es.	It's you (fam.).

Er ist es.	It's him (he).
Sie ist es.	It's her (she).
Wir sind es.	It's us (we).
Ihr seid es.	It's you (fam.).
Sie sind es.	It's you (polite).
Sie sind es.	It's they.

2. It's mine

Es ist meiner, (meine, meines).	It's mine.
Es ist dein (-er, -e, -es).	It's yours (fam.).
Es ist sein (-er, -e, -es).	It's his.
Es ist ihr (-er, -e, -es).	It's hers.
Es ist unser (-er, -e, -es).	It's ours.
Es ist eu (re). (-er, -e, -es).	It's yours (fam.).
Es ist Ihr (-er, -e, -es).	It's yours (polite).
Es ist ihr (-er, -e, -es).	It's theirs.

3. To me

Geben Sie es mir.	Give it to me.
Geben Sie es ihm.	Give it to him.
Geben Sie es uns.	Give it to us.
Geben Sie es ihnen.	Give it to them.
Geben Sie das.	Give it! Give this one (that one)!
Geben Sie das mir.	Give it to me.
Geben Sie das ihm.	Give it to him.
Geben Sie das uns.	Give it to us.
Geben Sie das ihnen.	Give it to them.

4. He speaks to me.

Er spricht mit mir.	He speaks to me.
Er spricht mit dir.	He speaks to you.

Er spricht mit ihm.	He speaks to him.
Er spricht mit uns.	He speaks to us.
Er spricht mit euch.	He speaks to you (fam.).
Er spricht mit Ihnen.	He speaks to you (polite).
Er spricht mit ihnen.	He speaks to them.

5. He gives it to me.

Er gibt es mir.	He gives it to me.
Er gibt es dir.	He gives it to you (fam.).
Er gibt es ihm.	He gives it to him.
Er gibt es uns.	He gives it to us.
Er gibt es Ihnen.	He gives it to you (polite).
Er gibt es ihnen.	He gives it to them.

6. About me.

Ich spreche von dir.	I'm talking about you (fam.).
Du sprichst von mir.	You're talking about me.
Er spricht von ihm.	He's talking about him.
Sie spricht von ihm.	She's talking about him.
Man spricht von ihr.	People are talking about her.
Wir sprechen von Ihnen.	We're talking about you (polite).
Sie sprechen von uns.	You're talking about us.
Sie sprechen von ihnen.	They're talking about them.

7. I Am Thinking of You.

Ich denke an dich.	I think of you.
Ich denke an ihn.	I think of him.

Du denkst an sie.	You're thinking of her.
Er denkt an uns.	He is thinking of us.
Wir denken an Sie.	We're thinking of you (polite).

32. MYSELF, YOURSELF, HIMSELF

ich wasche mich	I wash myself
du wäschst dich	you wash yourself
er wäscht sich	he washes himself
sie wäscht sich	she washes herself
wir waschen uns	we wash ourselves
ihr wascht euch	you wash yourselves
Sie waschen sich	you wash yourselves
sie waschen sich	they wash themselves

Notice that myself, yourself, etc. is *mich, dich,* etc.
Verbs that take *mich, dich,* etc. are called reflexive
verbs. A number of verbs that do not take "myself,
yourself," etc. in English, do so in German:

Ich setze mich.	I sit down.
Ich erhebe mich.	I get up ("I raise myself").
Ich erinnere mich.	I recall.
Ich freue mich.	I rejoice. I'm glad.
Ich irre mich.	I am mistaken.
Ich langweile mich.	I'm bored.
Ich unterhalte mich.	I'm having a good time.

QUIZ 10

1. Geben Sie ihr das.	1. I'm glad.
2. Er spricht von ihm.	2. I bought myself a hat.
3. Sie sprechen von ihnen.	3. My friends and your friends.
4. Er gibt es ihnen.	4. He washes himself.
5. Meine Freunde und Ihre Freunde.	5. I recall.

6. *Ich unterhalte mich.*	6. He gives it to them.
7. *Ich erinnere mich.*	7. I'm having a good time.
8. *Ich habe mir einen Hut gekauft.*	8. He's talking about him.
9. *Er wäscht sich.*	9. Give it to them.
10. *Ich freue mich.*	10. They're talking about them.

ANSWERS

1—9; 2—8; 3—10; 4—6; 5—3; 6—7; 7—5; 8—2; 9—4; 10—1.

WORD STUDY

Maus (die)	mouse
Garten (der)	garden
Mann (der)	man
Sohn (der)	son
jung	young
Freund (der)	friend
Busch (der)	bush
Fuchs (der)	fox
Fisch (der)	fish
bringen	(to) bring

LESSON 19

(Greeting and Leave-taking)

33. HELLO!

Guten Tag.
Hello. Good afternoon.

Guten Morgen.
Good morning.

Guten Tag, Herr Müller.
Hello, Mr. Müller. Good afternoon, Mr. Müller.

Wie geht es Ihnen?
How are you? How do you do? ("How is it going with you?")

Danke, gut. Danke, sehr gut.
Very well, thanks.

Nicht besonders.
So, so.

Und Ihnen? (Und wie geht es Ihnen?)
And you? ("And how are you?")

Nicht schlecht.
Not bad.

Nicht schlecht, danke.
Not bad, thanks.

Wie geht es?
How are you? How are things? ("How goes it?")

Danke, es geht.
All right, thank you. Fine. ("Thanks, it goes.")

Danke, es geht mir gut.
I am doing fine, thank you. ("Thanks, it goes well with me.")

34. I'D LIKE YOU TO MEET...

Gestatten Sie, dass ich Ihnen Frau Müller vorstelle.
Allow me to present ("to you") Mrs. Müller.

Gestatten Sie, dass ich Ihnen Herr Müller vorstelle.
Allow me to present ("to you") Mr. Müller.

Sehr erfreut.
Glad to know you. Glad to meet you. ("Very pleased.")

Sehr erfreut, Sie kennenzulernen, gnädige Frau.
Glad to know you madam ("gracious lady"). Glad to meet you ("to make your acquaintance").

Das ist Herr Müller.
This is Mr. Müller.
Sehr angenehm, Herr Müller.
Glad to know you, Mr. Müller. ("Very agreeable, Mr. Müller.")

35. HOW ARE THINGS?

Guten Tag.	Hello!
Wie geht's?	How are you? How are things? ("How goes it.")
Es geht gut, danke.	Fine, thanks.
Was gibt es Neues?	What's new?
Nicht viel.	Nothing much.
Rufen Sie mich in diesen Tagen an.	Phone me one of these days.
Vergessen Sie es nicht.	Don't forget.
Ich werde es bestimmt tun.	I'll certainly do so.
Sicher?	You're sure? ("Surely?")
Ganz bestimmt.	Sure! ("Quite certain.")
Bis demnächst.	See you soon. ("Until the next time.")
Bis gleich.	See you soon. See you in a little while.
Bis Montag.	Till Monday. See you Monday.
Bis morgen.	Till tomorrow. See you tomorrow.
Ich sehe Sie in einer Woche.	I'll see you in a week.
Ich sehe Sie in zwei Wochen.	I'll see you in two weeks.
Ich sehe Sie Freitag abend.	I'll see you Friday evening.

Ich sehe Sie nächsten Donnerstag.	I'll see you next Thursday.
Ich sehe Sie nächsten Donnerstag um acht Uhr abends.	I'll see you next Thursday at eight o'clock (in the evening).
Ich sehe Sie heute abend.	I'll see you this evening (tonight).

QUIZ 11

1. *Wie geht's?*	1. How are you? How do you do?
2. *Bis morgen.*	2. Very well, thanks.
3. *Sehr erfreut.*	3. Not too bad. ("Not bad.")
4. *Was gibt es Neues?*	4. How are you?
5. *Nun, was gibt es Neues?*	5. Until tomorrow.
6. *Es geht mir gut, danke.*	6. I'm happy to know you.
7. *Nichts Neues.*	7. What's new?
8. *Guten Tag.*	8. Well, what's new?
9. *Nicht schlecht.*	9. Good afternoon. Hello.
10. *Wie geht es Ihnen?*	10. Nothing much. ("Nothing new.")
11. *Bis gleich.*	11. Allow me . . .
12. *Rufen Sie mich in diesen Tagen an.*	12. Phone me one of these days.
13. *Bis demnächst.*	13. See you Monday. ("Until Monday.")
14. *Gestatten Sie mir . . .*	14. See you soon. ("Until the next time.")
15. *Bis Montag.*	15. See you soon. See you in a little while.

ANSWERS

1—4; 2—5; 3—6; 4—7; 5—8; 6—2; 7—10; 8—9;
9—3; 10—1; 11—15; 12—12; 13—14; 14—11;
15—13.

LESSON 20

(Introductions)

36. HAVE YOU TWO MET?

Kennen Sie meinen Freund?	Do you know my friend?
Nein, ich glaube nicht.	No, I don't think (believe) so.
Nein, ich habe nicht das Vergnügen.	No, I don't have the pleasure.
Ich glaube, Sie kennen sich schon?	I believe you already know each other.
Ja, wir haben uns schon kennen gelernt.	Yes, we've already met.
Nein, ich glaube nicht, dass wir uns schon kennen gelernt haben.	No, I don't believe we've met before.
Ich hatte bereits das Vergnügen . . .	I've already had the pleasure . . . (of meeting him)

37. GLAD TO HAVE MET YOU

Ich freue mich, Ihre Bekanntschaft gemacht zu haben.
Glad to have met you.

Ich hoffe, Sie bald wiederzusehen.
Hope to see you soon.

Ganz meinerseits.

The same here.

**Lassen Sie uns in den nächsten Tagen wieder
  zusammenkommen!**

Let's get together again one of these days!

Abgemacht!

Fine. ("Agreed.")

Haben Sie meine Adresse und Telefonnummer?

Do you have my address and telephone number?

Nein, geben Sie sie mir.

No, let me have them. ("Give them to me.")

**Meine Adresse ist Grosse Friedrichstrasse
  Nr. 21 (einundzwanzig).**

My address is 21 Grosse Friedrichstrasse.

**Meine Telefonnummer ist D. sieben
  einundachtzig zwölf.**

My telephone number is D. 7 8112.

Geben Sie mir bitte auch Ihre Geschäftsadresse.

Give me your business address, too, please.

**Ich schreibe es Ihnen auf, das ist
  Kurfürstendamm einhundertzwei.**

I'll write it for you. It's 102 Kurfürstendamm.

**Sie können mich zu Hause vor neun Uhr
  morgens anrufen.**

You can get me at home before nine in the
  morning.

Andernfalls im Büro.

Otherwise ("in the other case") at the office.

Gut, ich werde es nicht versäumen.

Good, I'll do that. ("Good, I won't fail to do so.")

**Auf Wiedersehen und vergessen Sie nicht
  anzurufen.**

Good-by, and don't forget to give me a ring.

**Nein, ich werde es nicht vergessen. Auf baldiges
  Wiedersehen! (Auf bald.)**

No, I won't forget. See you soon.

QUIZ 12

1. *Nein, ich glaube nicht.*
2. *Ja, wir haben uns schon kennen gelernt.*
3. *Nein, geben Sie sie mir.*
4. *Geben Sie mir auch ihre Geschäftsadresse.*
5. *Auf bald.*
6. *Gut, ich werde es nicht versäumen.*
7. *Haben Sie meine Adresse und meine Telefonnummer?*
8. *Nein, ich habe nicht das Vergnügen.*
9. *Ich hoffe Sie bald wiederzusehen.*
10. *Ich freue mich, Ihre Bekanntschaft gemacht zu haben.*

1. Yes, we've already met.
2. No, I don't have the pleasure.
3. No, I don't think (believe) so.
4. Glad to have met you.
5. I hope to see you soon.
6. Give me your business address too.
7. No, let me have them. ("Give them to me.")
8. Do you have my address and telephone number?
9. Good, I'll do that. ("Good, I won't fail to do so.")
10. Good-by. ("See you soon.")

ANSWERS

1—3; 2—1; 3—7; 4—6; 5—10; 6—9; 7—8; 8—2; 9—5; 10—4.

WORD STUDY

Huf (der)	hoof
Mond (der)	moon
Punkt (der)	point
Onkel (der)	uncle
Áfrika (das)	Africa

Ball (der)	ball
Wétter (das)	weather
Érde (die)	earth
Família (die)	family
Kóble (die)	coal

REVIEW QUIZ 2

1. *Würden Sie etwas langsamer* _____ (speak), *bitte.*
   a. *sagen*
   b. *sprechen*
   c. *wiederholen*

2. *Sprechen Sie* _____ (slowly), *bitte.*
   a. *schnell*
   b. *weniger*
   c. *langsam*

3. *Ich gebe dem Kind* _____ (the) *Buch.*
   a. *ein*
   b. *das*
   c. *die*

4. *Er gibt seiner Frau* _____ (a) *Brief.*
   a. *einen*
   b. *die*
   c. *der*

5. *Das ist nicht sebr* _____ (far).
   a. *weit*
   b. *hier*
   c. *dort*

6. *Er gibt* _____ (to the) *Armen Geld.*
   a. *die*
   b. *den*
   c. *ich*

7. *Ich* _____ (am) *in dem Zimmer.*
   a. *bist*
   b. *bin*
   c. *nicht*

8. *Er Kommt nicht* _____ (late).
   a. *bin*
   b. *Sie*
   c. *spät*

9. *Wo* _____ (are) *Ihre Bücher?*
   a. *seine*
   b. *sind*
   c. *ist*

10. _____ (Bring) *Sie mir ein Glas.*
    a. *Möchte*
    b. *Geben*
    c. *Bringen*

11. *Das ist* _____ (less) *schwer.*
    a. *weniger*
    b. *mehr*
    c. *nichts*

12. *Das ist* _____ (for) *die Kinder.*
    a. *ihr*
    b. *für*
    c. *durch*

13. *Ich* _____ (have) *kein Geld.*
    a. *habe*
    b. *haben*
    c. *nichts*

14. _____ (Have) *Sie Zigaretten?*
    a. *Hat*
    b. *Hast*
    c. *Haben*

15. *Ich* _____ (understand) *nicht gut Deutsch.*
    a. *verstehe*
    b. *spreche*
    c. *bitte*

16. *Ich* _____ (thank) *Ihnen vielmals.*
    a. *langsam*
    b. *danke*
    c. *verstehe*

17. *Ist er* _____ (here)?
    a. *wo*
    b. *dass*
    c. *hier*

18. *Sind sie* _____ (ready)?
    a. *wahr*
    b. *bereit*
    c. *wo*

19. *Ist das* _____ (true)?
    a. *bereit*
    b. *wahr*
    c. *wo*

20. *Ich ver stehe ein* _____ (little).
    a. *nur*
    b. *sehr*
    c. *wenig*

ANSWERS

1—b; 2—c; 3—b; 4—a; 5—a; 6—b; 7—b; 8—c; 9—b;
10—c; 11—a; 12—b; 13—a; 14—c; 15—a; 16—b;
17—c; 18—b; 19—b; 20—c.

LESSON 21

(Numbers I)

38. NUMBERS

1. One, Two, Three

eins	one
zwei	two
drei	three
vier	four
fünf	five
sechs	six
sieben	seven
acht	eight
neun	nine
zehn	ten
elf	eleven
zwölf	twelve
dreizehn	thirteen
vierzehn	fourteen
fünfzehn	fifteen
sechzehn	sixteen
siebzehn	seventeen
achtzehn	eighteen
neunzehn	nineteen
zwanzig	twenty
einundzwanzig	twenty-one
zweiundzwanzig	twenty-two
dreiundzwanzig	twenty-three
dreissig	thirty
einunddreissig	thirty-one
zweiunddreissig	thirty-two
dreiunddreissig	thirty-three

vierzig	forty
einundvierzig	forty-one
zweiundvierzig	forty-two
dreiundvierzig	forty-three
fünfzig	fifty
einundfünfzig	fifty-one
zweiundfünfzig	fifty-two
dreiundfünfzig	fifty-three
sechzig	sixty
einundsechzig	sixty-one
zweiundsechzig	sixty-two
dreiundsechzig	sixty-three
siebzig	seventy
einundsiebzig	seventy-one
zweiundsiebzig	seventy-two
dreiundsiebzig	seventy-three
achtzig	eighty
einundachtzig	eighty-one
zweiundachtzig	eighty-two
dreiundachtzig	eighty-three
neunzig	ninety
einundneunzig	ninety-one
zweiundneunzig	ninety-two
dreiundneunzig	ninety-three
hundert	a hundred
hunderteins	a hundred and one
hundertzwei	a hundred and two
hundertdrei	a hundred and three
tausend	a thousand
tausendeins	a thousand and one
tausendzwei	a thousand and two
tausenddrei	a thousand and three

LESSON 22

(Numbers II)

2. Some More Numbers

hundertzwanzig	a hundred and twenty
hundertzweiundzwanzig	a hundred and twenty-two
hundertdreissig	a hundred and thirty
hundertvierzig	a hundred and forty
hundertfünfzig	a hundred and fifty
hundertsechzig	a hundred and sixty
hundertsiebzig	a hundred and seventy
hunderteinundsiebzig	a hundred and seventy-one
hundertachtundsiebzig	a hundred and seventy-eight
hundertachtzig	a hundred and eighty
hundertneunzig	a hundred and ninety
hundertachtundneunzig	a hundred and ninety-eight
hundertneunundneunzig	a hundred and ninety-nine
zweihundert	two hundred
dreihundert-vierundzwanzig	three hundred and twenty-four
achthundert-fünfundsiebzig	eight hundred and seventy-five

3. First, Second, Third

1. erster, erste, erstes	first
2. zweiter (-e, -es)	second
3. dritter (-e, -es)	third
4. vierter (-e, -es)	fourth

5. fünfter (-e, -es)	fifth
6. sechster (-e, -es)	sixth
7. siebenter (-e, -es)	seventh
8. achter (-e, -es)	eighth
9. neunter (-e, -es)	ninth
10. zehnter (-e, -es)	tenth

das erste Buch	the first book
die erste Sache	the first thing
der zweite Akt	the second act
die dritte Klasse	the third class
die vierte Etage	the fourth floor
der fünfte Mann	the fifth man
der sechste Tag	the sixth day
die siebente Woche	the seventh week
der achte Monat	the eighth month
das neunte Jahr	the ninth year
Der zehnte Brief	the tenth letter
die elfte Person	the eleventh person
das zwolfte Kapitel	the twelfth chapter
der dreizehnte Gast	the thirteenth guest
das vierzehnte Paket	the fourteenth package
die fünfzehnte Tür	the fifteenth door
das sechzehnte Schiff	the sixteenth boat
die siebzehnte Strasse	the seventeenth street
die achtzehnte Ausgabe	the eighteenth edition
das neunzehnte Auto	the nineteenth car
das zwanzigste Haus	the twentieth house
der einundzwanzigste Januar	the twenty-first of January

QUIZ 13

1. sech Kilometer	1. the third class
2. zwei junge Mädchen	2. the eighth month
3. zwanzig Minuten	3. the ninth year
4. die dritte Klasse	4. six kilometers

5. *neunzehnter*
6. *die elfte Person*
7. *siebzehnter*
8. *der achte Monat*
9. *dreizehnter*
10. *das neunte Jahr*

5. two young girls
6. twenty minutes
7. the eleventh person
8. thirteenth
9. seventeenth
10. nineteenth

ANSWERS

1—4; 2—5; 3—6; 4—1; 5—10; 6—7; 7—9; 8—2; 9—8; 10—3.

4. Two and Two

Zwei und eins macht drei.
Two and one are ("makes") three.

Oder or

Zwei und eins sind drei.
Two and one are three.

Zwei und zwei macht vier.
Two and two are ("makes") four.

Oder or

Zwei und zwei sind vier.
Two and two are four.

Vier und drei macht sieben.
Four and three are ("makes") seven.

Fünf und zwei sind sieben.
Five and two are seven.

Sieben und eins macht acht.
Seven and one are ("makes") eight.

LESSON 23

(Currency, Telephone Numbers, Dates)

39. IT COSTS...

Das kostet...
This costs...

Das kostet fünf Mark.
This cost five marks.

Dieses Buch kostet zehn Mark fünfzig.
This book costs ten marks fifty pfennings.

**Dieser Hut hat mich vierundfünfzig Mark
gekostet.**
This hat cost me fifty-four marks.

**Ich habe zweihundert Mark für dieses Kleid
bezahlt.**
I paid two hundred marks for this dress.

**Ich habe diesen Wagen für zehntausend Mark
gekauft.**
I bought this car for ten thousand marks.

Das ist zwei Mark der Liter.
It's two marks a liter.

Das kostet fünfundzwanzig Mark der Meter.
That costs twenty-five marks a meter.

Der Preis ist zwölfhundert Mark.
The price is twelve hundred marks.

Sie kosten fünfzig Pfenning das Stück.
They cost fifty pfennings apiece.

40. THE TELEPHONE NUMBER IS...

Meine Telefonnummer ist Barbarossa 5 43 13
(fünf dreiundvierzig dreizehn).
My telephone number is Barbarossa 5 43 13.

Versuchen Sie die Nummer Mitte 2 21 12
(zwei einundzwanzig zwölf).
Try number Mitte 2 21 12.

Meine Telefonnummer ist geändert: sie ist jetzt Wannsee 5 3389
(fünf dreiunddreissig neunundachtzig).
My telephone number has been changed: it's now Wannsee 5 3389.

Ihre Telefonnummer ist Neuköln 4 60 91
(vier sechzig einundneunzig).
Their telephone number is Neuköln 4 60 91.

41. THE NUMBER IS ...

Ich wohne Leipzigerstrasse Nummer siebzehn.
I live at 17 Leipziger Street.

Er wohnt Schillerstrasse 4.
He lives at 4 Schiller Street.

Unsere Adresse ist Breitestrasse elf.
Our address is 11 Broad Street.

Wir wohnen in der Kaiserstrasse Nummer zweihundertdreiundsechzig.
We live at 263 Kaiser Street.

Meine Zimmernummer ist zweiundvierzig.
My room number is 42.

42. SOME DATES

Amerika wurde vierzehnhundertzweiundneunzig entdeckt.
America was discovered in 1492.

Das geschah achtzehnhunderteinundneunzig.
It happened in 1891.

Ich bin neunzehnhundertzwölf geboren.
I was born in 1912.

**Alles das geschah
neunzehnhundertvierundfünfzig.**
All this happened in 1954.

**Die New Yorker Weltausstellung fand
neunzehnhundertneunddreissig statt.**
The New York World's Fair took place in 1939.

Ich war neunzehnhundertfünfzig in Frankfurt.
I was in Frankfurt in 1950.

WORDS

mild	mild
Korn (das)	grain
reich	rich
Weg (der)	way
Million (die)	million
tausend	thousand
hundert	hundred
Hitze (die)	heat
heiss	hot
Konzert (das)	concert

QUIZ 14

1. *Das kostet fünf Mark.*
2. *Ihre Telefonnummer ist Mitte drei einundzwanzig vierzehn.*
3. *Ich habe diesen Wagen für sechstausend Mark gekauft.*
4. *Ich war neunzehnhunderteinundfünfzig in Berlin.*
5. *Sie kosten fünfzig pfennig das Stück.*

1. That costs five marks.
2. I bought this car for six thousand marks.
3. Their phone number is Mitte 3 21 14.
4. They cost fifty pfennigs each (a piece).
5. I was in Berlin in 1951.

ANSWERS

1—1; 2—3; 3—2; 4—5; 5—4.

LESSON 24

(Time I)

43. WHAT TIME IS IT?

Wie spät ist es?
What time is it?

Wieviel Uhr ist es, bitte?
Do you have the time, please?

Es ist ein Uhr.
It's one o'clock.

Es ist zwei Uhr.
It's two o'clock.

Es ist drei Uhr.
It's three o'clock.

Es ist vier Uhr.
It's four o'clock.

Es ist fünf Uhr.
It's five o'clock.

Es ist sechs Uhr.
It's six o'clock.

Es ist sieben Uhr.
It's seven o'clock.

Es ist acht Uhr.
It's eight o'clock.

Es ist neun Uhr.
It's nine o'clock.

Es ist zehn Uhr.
It's ten o'clock

Es ist elf Uhr.
It's eleven o'clock.

Es ist zwölf Uhr (Mittag).
It's twelve o'clock (noon).

Es ist dreizehn Uhr.
It's one P.M. ("thirteen o'clock").

Es ist vierzehn Uhr.
It's two P.M. ("fourteen o'clock").

Es ist fünfzehn Uhr.
It's three P.M. ("fifteen o'clock).

Es ist sechzehn Uhr.
It's four P.M. ("sixteen o'clock").

Es ist siebzehn Uhr.
It's five P.M. ("seventeen o'clock").

Es ist achtzehn Uhr.
It's six P.M. ("eighteen o'clock").

Es ist neunzehn Uhr.
It's seven P.M. ("nineteen o'clock").

Es ist zwanzig Uhr.
It's eight P.M. ("twenty o'clock").

Es ist einundzwanzig Uhr.
It's nine P.M. ("twenty-one o'clock").

Es ist zweiundzwanzig Uhr.
It's ten P.M. ("twenty-two o'clock").

Es ist dreiundzwanzig Uhr.
It's eleven P.M. ("twenty-three o'clock").

Es ist vierundzwanzig Uhr.
It's twelve P.M. ("twenty-four o'clock").

Es ist Mitternacht.
It's midnight.

When you want to specify whether you mean "seven A.M." or "seven P.M." you say *sieben Uhr morgens* ("seven hours of the morning") or *vormittags Sieben Uhr abends* ("seven hours of the evening") or *nachmittags*.

Official time (formal announcements of meetings,

timetables, etc.) is on a twenty-four hour basis, like our Army time. Thus, in a formal announcement you may see *siebzehn Uhr dreissig* for 5:30 P.M. Ordinarily, however, you say *fünf Uhr dreissig* or *halb sechs nachmittags*—that is, instead of our "A.M." and "P.M." you add, as necessary, *morgens, nachmittags* or *abends*.

44. THE TIME IS NOW

Die Sekunde	second
Die Minute	minute
Die Stunde	hour

Es ist viertel nach zwei.
It's a quarter after two.

Es ist zwei Uhr fünfzehn.
It's two-fifteen.

Es ist viertel vor vier.
It's a quarter to four.

Es ist drei Uhr fünfundvierzig.
It's three forty-five.

Es ist halb drei.
It's half past two.

Es ist zwei Uhr dreissig.
It's two-thirty.

Es ist zwanzig vor fünf.
It's twenty to five.

Es ist neun Uhr fünfunddreissig.
It's nine thirty-five.

Es ist Mittag.
It's noon.

Es ist fünf vor zwölf.
It's five to twelve.

Es ist fünf nach zwölf.
It's five past twelve.

Es ist ein Uhr morgens.
It's one o'clock in the morning.

Es ist ungefähr fünf Uhr.
It's about five.

Es ist fast elf Uhr.
It's almost eleven.

Es ist erst halb sieben.
It's only half past six.

Es ist fünf Uhr durch.
It's after five.

45. A MATTER OF TIME

Wann kommen Sie? Um wieviel Uhr kommen Sie?
When will you come? What time will you come?

Ich werde um drei Uhr dort sein.
I'll be there (at) three o'clock.

Sie ist um zwanzig vor drei gekommen.
She came at twenty to three.

Er wird um zwei Uhr nachmittags kommen.
He'll come at two P.M.

Wir werden gegen neun Uhr fünfundzwanzig dort sein.
We'll be there about nine twenty-five.

Er wird um zehn Uhr dreissig heute abend zurückkommen.
He'll be back at ten-thirty tonight.

Ich werde Sie dort gegen Viertel nach acht sehen.
I'll see you there about ("toward") eight-fifteen.

Wir treffen uns um sechs.
We'll meet at six.

Ich gehe um vier Uhr aus.
I'm going out at four o'clock.

Kommen Sie zwischen sieben und acht.
Come between seven and eight.

Er kommt um sechs Uhr abends.
He'll come at six in the evening.
Kommen Sie um zehn Uhr heute abend.
Come at ten o'clock tonight.

Der Zug fährt um neun Uhr vierzig ab.
The train leaves at nine-forty.

WORD STUDY

hoffen	(to) hope
Distanz (die)	distance
Quantität (die)	quantity
Seite (die)	side
Welt (die)	world
Jahr (das)	year
Krone (die)	crown
Pflanze (die)	plant
Kredit (der)	credit
wandern	(to) wander

QUIZ 15

1. *Es ist halb drei.*
2. *Es ist Viertel nach zwei.*
3. *Es ist neun Uhr fünfunddreissig.*
4. *Kommen Sie zwischen sieben und acht.*
5. *Ich werde Sie dort gegen Viertel nach acht sehen.*
6. *Der Zug kommt um sieben Uhr dreiundzwanzig an.*
7. *Kommen Sie gegen zehn Uhr heute abend.*
8. *Es ist ein Uhr morgens.*
9. *Wir werden gegen neun Uhr fünfundzwanzig dort sein.*
10. *Er kommt um zwei Uhr nachmittags.*

1. I'll see you there about eight-fifteen.
2. The train arrives at seven twenty-three.
3. Come between seven and eight.

4. Come at ten o'clock tonight.
5. It's one o'clock in the morning.
6. He'll come at two P.M.
7. We'll be there about nine twenty-five.
8. It's two-fifteen. It's a quarter after two.
9. It's half past two. It's two-thirty.
10. It's nine thirty-five.

ANSWERS

1—9; 2—8; 3—10; 4—3; 5—1; 6—2; 7—4; 8—5;
9—7; 10—6.

LESSON 25

(Time II)

46. IT'S TIME

Es ist Zeit.
It's time.

Es ist Zeit, es zu tun.
It's time to do it.

Es ist Zeit zu gehen.
It's time to leave.

Es ist Zeit, nach Hause zu gehen.
It's time to go home.

Ich habe Zeit.
I have time.

Ich habe genug Zeit.
I have enough time.

Ich habe keine Zeit.
I haven't any time.

Wie lange beabsichtigen Sie, hier zu bleiben?
How long do you intend to stay here?

Seit wann sind Sie hier?
How long have you been here?
Er verliert seine Zeit.
He's wasting his time.

Geben Sie ihm Zeit, es zu tun.
Give him time to do it.

Gib mir Zeit, mich anzuziehen.
Just give me enough time to get dressed.

Er kommt von Zeit zu Zeit.
He comes from time to time.

47. MORNING, NOON AND NIGHT

der Morgen	morning
der Mittag	noon
der Nachmittag	afternoon
der Abend	evening
die Nacht	night
der Tag	the day
die Wache	the week
acht Tage	a week ("eight days")
vierzehn Tage	two weeks ("fourteen days")
der Monat	the month
das Jahr	the year
gestern	yesterday
heute	today
morgen	tomorrow
vorgestern	the day before yesterday
übermorgen	the day after tomorrow
vor kurzem	a while ago
jetzt	now
einen Augenblick	in a moment
lange her	a long time ago
kürzlich	a little while ago

heute morgen	this morning
gestern morgen	yesterday morning
morgen früh	tomorrow morning
heute nachmittag	this afternoon
gestern nachmittag	yesterday afternoon
morgen nachmittag	tomorrow afternoon
heute abend	this evening
gestern abend	last evening
morgen abend	tomorrow evening
heute nacht	tonight
gestern nacht	last night
morgen nacht	tomorrow night

LESSON 26

(Time III)

diese Woche
this week

vorige Woche
last week

nächste Woche
next week

in zwei Wochen
in two weeks, the week after next

vor zwei Wochen
two weeks ago, the week before last

dieser Monat
this month

der vorige Monat
last month

der nächste Monat
next month

in zwei Monaten
in two months, the month after next

vor zwei Monaten
two months ago, the month before last

dieses Jahr
this year

voriges Jahr
last year

nächstes Jahr
next year

in zwei Jahren
in two years, the year after next

vor zwei Jahren
two years ago, the year before last

am Morgen
in the morning

am Abend
in the evening

gegen Mittag
towards noon

nach dem Essen (Abendessen)
after dinner

am Ende der Woche
at the end of the week

am Monatsende
at the end of the month

gegen Wochenende
toward the end of the week

vor einer Stunde
an hour ago

in einer Viertelstunde
in a quarter of an hour

dieser Tage
one of these days

alle Tage
every day

den ganzen Tag
all day (long)

die ganze Nacht
all night (long)

Er arbeitet von morgens bis abends.
He works from morning to night.

Was für ein Datum ist heute?
What's the date? ("today")

48. PAST, PRESENT AND FUTURE

Vergangenheit	*Gegenwart*	*Zukunft*
Past	Present	Future
Vor einem Augenblick	*In diesem Augenblick*	*im nächsten Augenblick*
a moment ago	now	in a moment, soon
gestern morgen	*heute morgen*	*morgen früh*
yesterday morning	this morning	tomorrow morning
gestern nachmittag	*heute nachmittag*	*morgen nachmittag*
yesterday afternoon	this afternoon	tomorrow afternoon
gestern abend	*heute abend*	*morgen abend*
last evening, last night	this evening, tonight	tomorrow evening, tomorrow night
vorige Woche	*diese Woche*	*nachste Woche*
last week	this week	next week
vorigen Monat	*diesen Monat*	*nächsten Monat*
last month	this month	next month
voriges Jahr	*dieses Jahr*	*nächstes Jahr*
last year	this year	next year

LESSON 27

(Days, Months, Seasons)

49. THE DAYS OF THE WEEK

Montag	Monday
Dienstag	Tuesday
Mittwoch	Wednesday
Donnerstag	Thursday
Freitag	Friday
Samstag, or *Sonnabend*	Saturday
Sonntag	Sunday

50. WHAT'S THE DATE TODAY?

The following expressions are all used for "What's the date today?"

Der wievielte ist heute?
"The how many is it?"

Welches Datum ist heute?
"What date is today?"

Den wievielten haben wir heute?
"The how many do we have today?"

Der wievielte ist Samstag?
What's the date Saturday?

Heute ist der zehnte.
Today's the tenth.

Heute haben wir den zwanzigsten.
Today is ("we have") the twentieth.

Ist heute Dienstag oder Mittwach?
Is today Tuesday or Wednesday?

Heute ist Mittwoch.
Today is Wednesday.

Heute ist Montag.
Today is Monday.

Kommen Sie nächsten Samstag.
Come next Saturday.
Er fährt nächsten Dienstag fort.
He's leaving next Tuesday.
Er ist letzten Montag angekommen.
He arrived last Monday.
Er kommt nächsten Montag an.
He's arriving next Monday.

QUIZ 16

1.	*vorgestern*	1.	afternoon
2.	*heute*	2.	day before yesterday
3.	*nachmittag*	3.	today
4.	*vor kurzem*	4.	day after tomorrow
5.	*morgen nachmittag*	5.	a while ago
6.	*heute nachmittag*	6.	tomorrow afternoon
7.	*übermorgen*	7.	this evening
8.	*Er verliert seine Zeit.*	8.	He's wasting his time.
9.	*heute nacht*	9.	this afternoon
10.	*Seit wann sind Sie hier?*	10.	How long have you been here?
11.	*nächste Woche*	11.	in two months, the month after next
12.	*vorige Woche*	12.	two weeks ago, the week before last
13.	*vor zwei Wochen*	13.	next week
14.	*in zwei Monaten*	14.	two years ago, the year before last
15.	*vor zwei Jahren*	15.	last week
16.	*Es ist Zeit*	16.	It's time to go home
17.	*Ich habe Zeit.*	17.	tomorrow night
18.	*Es ist Zeit, nach Hause zu gehen.*	18.	tonight
19.	*morgen abend*	19.	It's time.
20.	*heute abend*	20.	I have time.

ANSWERS

1—2; 2—3; 3—1; 4—5; 5—6; 6—9; 7—4; 8—8;
9—18; 10—10; 11—13; 12—15; 13—12; 14—11;
15—14; 16—19; 17—20; 18—16; 19—17; 20—7.

51. THE MONTHS

Jánuar	January
Február	February
März	March
Apríl	April
Mai	May
Júni	June
Júli	July
Augúst	August
Septémber	September
Október	October
Novémber	November
Dezémber	December

Heute ist der erste Juni.
Today is the first of June.

Ich wurde am zwölften April geboren.
I was born (on) April 12.

Meine Schwester wurde am fünften Mai geboren.
My sister was born (on) May 5.

Mein Geburtstag ist am zweiten Februar.
My birthday is (on) February 2.

Ich komme am vierzehnten Juli.
I'll come (on) the fourteenth of July.

Die Schule beginnt am zwanzigsten September.
School begins (on) the twentieth of September.

Ich bin am zweiundzwanzigsten März zurück.
I'll be back (on) March 22.

Der erste Januar ist ein Feiertag.
January 1 is a holiday.

Er fährt am sechsten Juli ab.
He's leaving (on) July 6.

Der Brief ist vom neunten Juni.
The letter is dated June 9.

Wir besuchen Sie am elften Mai.
We'll come to see you (on) May 11.

**Heute ist der zweite Mai,
neunzehnhundertsechsundfünfzig.**
Today is May 2, 1956.

52. THE SEASONS

der Frühling	spring
der Sommer	summer
der Herbst	autumn
der Winter	winter
im Winter	in winter
im Sommer	in summer
im Herbst	in autumn, in the fall
im Frühling	in spring

QUIZ 17

1. *Welches Datum ist heute?*
2. *bis dieser Tage*
3. *den ganzen Tag*
4. *im Sommer*
5. *in einer Viertelstunde*
6. *Er kommt nächsten Montag an.*
7. *Heute ist Montag.*
8. *Kommen Sie nächsten Samstag.*
9. *der Winter*
10. *Sonntag*
11. *Wir haben heute den zwanzigsten.*
12. *Der wievielte ist Samstag?*
13. *Ich komme am vierzehnten Juli.*
14. *Heute ist der erste Juni.*
15. *Der Brief ist vom sechsten Juni.*

1. Sunday
2. in a quarter of an hour
3. See you one of these days.
4. all day
5. What's today
6. in the summer
7. winter
8. What's the date Saturday?
9. Today's the twentieth.
10. Today's Monday.
11. Come next Saturday.
12. He'll arrive next Monday.
13. The letter is dated June 6.
14. I'll come (on) the fourteenth of July.
15. Today is the first of June.

ANSWERS

1—5; 2—3; 3—4; 4—6; 5—2; 6—12; 7—10; 8—11;
9—7; 10—1; 11—9; 12—8; 13—14; 14—15; 15—13.

WORD STUDY

Féuer	*(das)*	fire
Grammátik	*(die)*	grammar
Súppe	*(die)*	soup
Sack	*(der)*	sack
füllen		(to) fill
Argumént	*(das)*	argument
Monumént	*(das)*	monument
flach		flat
dick		thick
Stein	*(der)*	stone

Vor dem Zeitungsstand
(At the Newsstand)

*"Fräulein, geben Sie mir Die Welt, bitte. Ich habe
nur kein Kleingeld. Können Sie mir hundert
Mark wechseln?"*

"Miss, give me *Die Welt*, please. However, I don't
have any small change. Can you change a
hundred marks for me?"

*"Geben Sie mir die zwanzig pfennig morgen,"
sagte die Verkäuferin.*

"Give me the twenty *pfennig* tomorrow," the
saleslady said.

*"Aber angenommen ich werde heute abend
überfahren?"*

"But suppose I get run over tonight?"

*"Na wenn schon! Das wäre doch kein grosser
Verlust!"*

"So what! It wouldn't be much of a loss!"

NOTES:

1. *Geld:* Money *Kleingeld:* change ("small
   money") *wechseln:* to change
2. *ein Mark* is 100 *Pfennig.*
3. *Verkäuferin*—saleslady
   Verkäufer—salesman
4. *überfahren:* run over ("driven over"); also
   infinitive ("to drive over")
5. *Na, wenn schon*—So what! ("Well, if so")

LESSON 28

(To Go)

53. TO GO

gehen to go (to travel by rail, by air, by boat) (by
foot)

ich gehe	I go
du gehst	you go
er geht (sie, es)	he goes
wir gehen	we go
ihr geht	you go
Sie gehen	you go
sie gehen	they go

2. Some Common Expressions with *gehen:*

Geh!	*Gehen Sie weiter!*
Go! (fam.)	Go on! Keep going!
Gehen Sie!	*Gehen Sie es suchen.*
Go!	Go look for it! Go get it!
Gehen Sie langsam.	*Wo gehen Sie hin?*
Go slowly.	Where are you going?
Gehen Sie nicht dorthin.	*Wir müssen dorthin gehen.*
Don't go there.	We have to go there. ("We must go there.")
Gehen Sie nicht dort hinüber.	*Ich gehe zum Bannhof.*
Don't go over there.	I'm going to the station.

Ich gehe zur Bank.
I'm going to the bank.

Ich gehe ins Theater.
I'm going to the theater.

Er geht aufs Land.
He's going to the country.

Ich gehe Hans besuchen.
I'm going to John's place (home). ("I'm going to visit Hans.")

Wie geht es Ihnen?
How are you? ("How goes it with you?")

Es geht mir gut.
Well, thanks. Fine, thanks.

Wie geht's?
How are you? How are things?

Gut. Danke.
Fine. All right. O.K.

2. When speaking of a trip, you may also use the verb *fahren*.

Wo fahren wir hin?
Where are we going?

Wohin fährst du?
Where are you going?

Wohin fährt er?
Where is he going?

Sie fährt nach Berlin
She is going to Berlin.

Wohin fahren wir?
Where are we going?

Wohin fahren Sie?
Where are you going?

Fahrt ihr nach Berlin?
Are you going to Berlin?

Nein, wir fahren nach Frankfurt.
No, we are going to Frankfurt.

Wohin fahren sie?
Where are they going?

54. A FEW SHORT PHRASES

Achtung!
Watch out! Pay attention!

Bis später.
See you later.

Obacht! Vorsicht!	**Beeilen Sie sich.**
Be careful! Watch out!	Hurry up.
Schnell.	**Beeilen Sie sich nicht.**
Fast.	Don't hurry up.
Schneller.	**Ich habe es eilig.**
Faster.	I'm in a hurry.
Nicht so schnell.	**Ich habe es nicht eilig.**
Not so fast.	I'm not in a hurry.
Nicht zu schnell.	**Lassen Sie sich Zeit.**
Not too fast.	Take your time.
Langsamer.	**Einen Moment!**
More slowly.	Just a minute!
Früher.	**Sofort.**
Sooner.	Right away.
Später.	**Bald.**
Later.	Soon.
Ich komme.	**Ich komme sofort.**
I'm coming.	I'm coming right away.

LESSON 29

(One, They, People, Little, Lot, More, Less)

55. ONE, THEY, PEOPLE

Man.
One. They. People.
Man sagt, dass . . .
They say that . . . It's said that . . . People say
  that . . .
Man hat mir gesagt, dass . . .
I've been told that . . .

Man sagt es.
They say it.

Man sagt, dass es wahr ist.
They say it's true.

Man hat mir gesagt.
I've been told.

Man weiss es nicht.
Nobody knows.

Man spricht Deutsch.
German spoken.

Hier spricht man Englisch.
English spoken here.

Spricht man Englisch hier?
Do they speak English here?

Wie sagt man das auf Deutsch?
How do you say that in German?

Wie sagt man "Good morning" auf Deutsch?
How do you say "Good morning" in German?

Wie schreibt man dieses Wort auf Deutsch?
How is this word written (spelled) in German?

Man läutet.
Someone's ringing.

Man schliesst.
They're closing

Was spielt man heute abend im Theater?
What's playing at the theater tonight?

Notice that *man* can often be translated by the English passive:

Man sagt, dass...
It's said that ...

Man hat mir gesagt, dass...
I've been told that ...

Wie schreibt man dieses Wort?
How is this word written?

QUIZ 18

1.	*Ich habe es eilig.*	1.	Right away.
2.	*Ich komme sofort.*	2.	In a minute.
3.	*Einen Moment.*	3.	I'm in a hurry.
4.	*Sofort.*	4.	I'm coming right away.
5.	*Lassen Sie sich Zeit.*	5.	Someone's ringing.
6.	*Man läutet.*	6.	Take your time.
7.	*Man hat mir gesagt.*	7.	Nobody knows.
8.	*Man weiss es nicht.*	8.	I've been told.
9.	*Hier spricht man Englisch.*	9.	How do you say that in German?
10.	*Wie sagt man das auf Deutsch?*	10.	English spoken here.

ANSWERS

1—3; 2—4; 3—2; 4—1; 5—6; 6—5; 7—8; 8—7; 9—10; 10-9.

WORD STUDY

Kórridor (der)	corridor
Lógik (die)	logic
tánzen	(to) dance
privát	private
Preis (der)	price
Széne (die)	scene
frei	free
modérn	modern
nämlich	namely
Náme (der)	name

56. A LITTLE AND A LOT

wenig
a little

viel oder wenig
a lot or a little

ein wenig
a little

sehr wenig
very little

ein klein wenig
a very little

ein ganz klein wenig
a very little bit

allmählich
little by little

Das ist zu wenig.
It's not enough.

noch ein wenig
a little bit more

Er spricht wenig.
He doesn't talk much.

Wollen Sie viel oder wenig davon?
Do you want a lot of it or a little?

Bleiben wir ein wenig hier.
Let's stay here a little.

Geben Sie mir ein wenig davon.
Give me a little of it.

Geben Sie mir ein wenig Wasser.
Give me a little water.

Ich spreche sebr wenig Deutsch.
I speak very little German.

viel
much, a lot

Ich habe nicht viel Geld.
I haven't much money.

Ich habe nicht viel Zeit.
I haven't much time.

Ich mag ihn sehr.
I like him (her, it) a lot.

Ich habe viel zu tun.
I have a lot to do.

57. TOO MUCH

Zu viel.
Too. Too much.

Das ist zu viel.
It's too much.

Das ist nicht zu viel.
That is not too much.

zu wenig
too little

zu heiss
too hot

zu kalt
too cold

zu viel Wasser
too much water

58. MORE OR LESS

mehr oder weniger
more or less

höchstens
at the most

wenigstens
at the least

mehr und mehr
more and more

immer weniger
less and less

sechs mal mehr
six times more

Es gibt nichts mehr davon.
There's no more of it.

Es ist mehr als das.
It's more than that.

Das ist das meist gelesene Buch, das ich kenne.
This is the most popular book I know.
   ("This is the most read book I know.")

59. ENOUGH AND SOME MORE

genug
enough

noch
some more

Ist es genug?
Is it enough?

Noch mehr? Noch etwas?
Some more?

Das ist genug.
It's enough.

noch ein wenig
a little more, another little bit

Das ist mehr als genug.
It's more than enough.

noch ein Glas Wasser
another glass of water

Das ist nicht genug.
That is not enough.

noch mehr Brot
some more bread

Das ist gross genug.
That's large enough.
That's rather large.

noch etwas Fleisch
some more meat

gut genug
fairly well, rather well

noch viel mehr
much more, lots more

Haben Sie genug Geld?
Do you have enough money?

Kommen Sie noch einmal.
Come again.

Sagen Sie es noch einmal.
Say it again.

Wiederholen Sie, bitte, noch einmal.
Please repeat it again.

60. GOOD

Das ist gut.
That's good.

Das ist sehr gut.
That's very good.

Das ist nicht gut.
That's not good.

Der Wein ist gut.
This wine is good.

Das Fleisch ist gut.
This meat is good.

Sie sind gut.
They're good.

Guten Tag!
Hello! Good afternoon. Good day.

Guten Abend!
Good evening!

Gute Nacht.
Good night.

61. GOOD, WELL

gut
good, well

Das ist sehr gut.
It's very good.

Das ist nicht gut.
That's not very good.

nicht zu gut
not too good

Sehr gut, mein Herr.
Very well, sir.

Ist es gut?
Is it good?

Das ist gut gemacht.
That's well done. ("well made")

Alles geht gut.
Everything's going well. Everything's all right.

Viel besser.
Much better.

QUIZ 19

1. *Alles geht gut.*
2. *Das ist sehr gut.*
3. *Ist es gut?*
4. *Das ist zu gut.*
5. *Haben Sie genug davon?*
6. *Sagen Sie es noch einmal.*
7. *Wiederholen Sie, bitte, noch einmal.*
8. *Kommen Sie noch einmal.*
9. *Ich mag es sehr.*
10. *Geben Sie mir ein wenig davon.*

1. That's very good.
2. Do you have enough of it?
3. Say it again.
4. Give me a little of it.
5. I like it a lot.
6. That's too good.
7. Everything is going well. Everything's all right.
8. Is it good?
9. Please repeat it.
10. Come again.

ANSWERS

1—7; 2—1; 3—8; 4—6; 5—2; 6—3; 7—9; 8—10;
9—5; 10—4.

WORD STUDY

nervós	nervous
Episóde (die)	episode
Summe (die)	sum
meinen	(to) mean, think (believe)
natürlich	natural
Nagel (der)	nail
elektrisch	electrical
Braut (die)	bride
Zeremonie (die)	ceremony
Wúnde (die)	wound

62. BEAUTIFUL

schön
beautiful

Es ist sehr schön.
It's very beautiful.

nicht sehr schön
not very beautiful

schönes Wetter
nice weather

ein schönes Land
a beautiful country

ein schöner Tag
a nice day

Es ist schön.
It's nice out.

schöne Künste
fine arts

schön und gut
well and good

63. LIKE, AS

wie
like, as

wie ich
like me

wie das
like this (that)

wie die andern
like the others

nicht so wie das
not like this (that)

wie dieses
like this

wie Sie wünschen
as you wish

Wie früh es ist!
How early (it is)!

Wie spät es ist!
How late (it is)!

Wie teuer das ist!
How expensive this is!

64. ALL, EACH, EVERY, WHOLE, ENTIRE

all, alles
all

jeder, jede, jedes
every, each

all und jeder
each and every

jeder Mensch
every human being

jeder Mann
every man, each man

jede Frau
every woman, each woman

jedes Kind
every child, each child

alle Menschen
all human beings

alle Männer
all men

alle Frauen
all women

jeder, jedermann
everybody, everyone

Alles ist hier.
Everything's here.

den ganzen Tag
all day long ("the whole day")

alle Tage
every day

Alles ist fertig.
Everything's ready.

Alle sind fertig.
All are ready.

Nehmen Sie sie alle.
Take all of them.

Wir sind alle da.
We're all here.

Das ist alles.
That's all. That's the whole lot. That'll do.

Ist das alles?
Is that all? Is that everything? Is that the whole lot?

alle
everybody (all of them)

Jeder weiss es.
Everybody knows it.

ganz
entire, entirely; complete, completely; whole,
  wholly

ganz schlecht
completely bad

Ganz und gar nicht.
Not at all.

Überhaupt nicht.
Not at all.

65. COMBINATIONS WITH *DAS;* SOME, ANY, SOMETHING, ANYTHING, NOTHING

Das is often combined with a preposition to form the
following expressions:

davon:	of it, of that
darin:	in it, in them
daran:	at it, at them
darüber:	about/over it, about/over them

darunter:	among/under it, among/under them
dadurch:	through it, through them
dazu:	to it, to them
dafür:	for it, for them
daraus:	from/out of it, from/out of them

Hier is die Tafel Schokolade, geben Sie jedem Kind ein Stück davon.

"Here is the chocolate bar. Give each child a piece of it."

Sie gab mir eine Pfeife, was soll ich damit tun?
"She gave me a pipe. What should I do with it?"

Bitte nehmen Sie dieses Buch, wir haben schon darüber gesprochen.
"Please take this book. We have already spoken about it."

etwas
some, any

Hat er etwas Geld?
Does he have any money?

Ja, er hat etwas.
Yes, he has some.

Haben Sie (etwas) Geld?
Do you have any money?

Nein, ich habe keins.
No, I don't have any.

Ist noch etwas von dem guten Wein übrig?
Is there (still) anything left of the good wine?

Nein, es ist nichts mehr davon übrig.
No, there is nothing (more) left of it.

Hier ist etwas Geld. Geben Sie Hans etwas davon.
Here's some money. Give some of it to John.

Ich habe genug davon.
I have enough of it.

Geben Sie mir etwas!
Give me something!

Geben Sie uns etwas davon!
Give us some of it!

Geben Sie ihm etwas!
Give him something!

Geben Sie ihnen nichts mehr davon.
Don't give them any more of it.

Ich habe ihm etwas davon gegeben.
I gave him some of it.

Geben Sie ihr nichts!
Don't give her anything! (Give her nothing)!

Ich habe mit ihr darüber gesprochen.
I spoke to her about it.

Kommt er aus Deutschland?
Does he come from Germany?
Is he coming from Germany?

Ja, er kommt direkt daher.
Yes, he is coming directly from there.

Es gibt etwas.
There is something.

Gibt es noch etwas davon?
Is (are) there any more of it?

Was halten Sie davon?
What do you think of (about) it?

QUIZ 20

1. *Gibt es noch etwas davon?*
2. *Es gibt etwas.*
3. *Haben Sie etwas Geld?*

1. It's very beautiful (nice, fine).
2. Nice weather.
3. A nice day.

4. *Haben Sie etwas davon?*	4. It's nice out. The weather's nice.
5. *Geben Sie ihm etwas mehr davon.*	5. A beautiful country.
6. *Geben Sie mir etwas.*	6. I gave him something.
7. *Nein, sie haben nichts.*	7. It's good.
8. *Was halten Sie davon?*	8. Do you have any?
9. *Ich habe ihm etwas gegeben.*	9. Do you have any money?
10. *Das ist gut.*	10. Give me something.
11. *Ein schönes Land.*	11. Give him some more of it.
12. *Schönes Wetter.*	12. There is something.
13. *Das ist sehr schön.*	13. Is (are) there more of it?
14. *Das Wetter ist schön.*	14. No, they haven't any.
15. *Ein schöner Tag.*	15. What do you think of it?

ANSWERS

1—13; 2—12; 3—9; 4—8; 5—11; 6—10; 7—14;
8—15; 9—6; 10—7; 11—5; 12—2; 13—1; 14—4;
15—3.

LESSON 30

(Same, Self, Already)

66. SMALL TALK

Aber sicher!
Of course! Certainly!

Einverstanden!
Of course! Agreed!

Das versteht sich.
Of course. Naturally. Certainly.

Tatsächlich? Wirklich?
Indeed? In fact? Really? (as a statement:
    "That's so. That's true.")

Um so schlimmer.
So much the worse.

Um so besser.
So much the better.

Ich denke ja!
I think so.

In Ordnung.
Agreed!

Ich bin einverstanden.
I agree.

Ich nehme es an.
I suppose so.

Ich nehme es nicht an.
I suppose not.

Ich hoffe.
I hope so.

Ich hoffe nicht.
I hope not.

Vielleicht.
Perhaps.

Natürlich.
Naturally.

Sicher, Sicherlich.
Certainly.

Sicher nicht.
Certainly not.

Das ist schade!
It's a pity! It's a shame! Too bad!

Wie schade!
What a pity! What a shame!

Das hängt davon ab.
That depends.

Das macht nichts.
That's nothing. That's not important. That doesn't
   matter.

Das macht garnichts.
That doesn't matter at all.

Das macht mir nichts aus.
It doesn't matter to me. I don't care.

Wenn es Ihnen nichts ausmacht
If you have no objection
If it doesn't inconvenience you

Das ist mir gleich.
I don't care. It's all the same to me.

QUIZ 21

1. *Das ist schade.*	1. Of course, certainly.
2. *Das macht nichts.*	2. I agree.
3. *Das macht mir nichts aus.*	3. Of course.
4. *Das hängt davon ab.*	4. Agreed!
5. *Einverstanden.*	5. I suppose so.
6. *Ich bin einverstanden*	6. I hope so.
7. *Ich hoffe.*	7. It's a pity (shame). Too bad!
8. *Aber sicher.*	8. That depends.

9. *In Ordnung.*

9. That's nothing. That's not important. That doesn't matter.

10. *Ich nehme es an.*

10. I don't care. It doesn't matter to me.

ANSWERS

1—7; 2—9; 3—10; 4—8; 5—3; 6—2; 7—6; 8—1; 9—4; 10—5.

67. THE SAME, MYSELF

dasselbe *(derselbe, dieselbe)*
the same

Das ist dasselbe.
That's the same thing.

Das sind nicht dieselben.
These aren't the same.

zur selben Zeit
at the same time

im (in dem) selben Augenblick
at the same moment

in derselben Stadt
in the same town

selbst
myself, yourself, etc.

Ich mache es selbst.
I'm doing it myself.

Du machst es selbst.
You're doing it yourself.

Er macht es selbst.
He's doing it himself.

Wir machen es selbst.
We're doing it ourselves.

Ihr macht es selbst.
You're doing it yourselves.

Sie machen es selbst.
You're doing it yourself.

Sie machen es selbst.
They are doing it themselves.

68. ALREADY

Schon.
Already.

Er ist schon da.
He's already here.

Er ist noch nicht da.
He is not here yet.

Er hat es schon getan.
He's already done that.

Ist er schon fort?
Has he left already?

Nein, er ist noch da (hier).
No, he is still here.

Er ist noch nicht fort.
He hasn't left yet.

Sind Sie schon fertig?
Have you finished already?

WORD STUDY

Milch (die)	milk
Stahl (der)	steel
Zinn (das)	tin
Sturm (der)	storm
Wolle (die)	wool
Öl (das)	oil
Sand (der)	sand
Eis (das)	ice
Amerika (das)	America
Finger (der)	finger

69. LIKING AND DISLIKING

1. I Like It

Gut!
Good!

Das ist gut.
It's good.

Das ist sehr gut.
It's very good.

Das gefällt mir sehr.
I like that very much.

Es gefällt mir grossartig.
It's grand. I like it a great deal.

Er ist sehr nett.
He's very nice.

Er ist sehr liebenswürdig.
He is very kind (amiable).

Sie sind sehr liebenswürdig.
You're very kind. That's very kind of you.

Das ist schön.
That's beautiful.

Das ist ausgezeichnet.
That's excellent.

Das ist hervorragend.
That's excellent. It's wonderful.

Das ist bewundernswert.
That's admirable. It's wonderful.

Das ist nett.
That's very nice. It's charming. It's lovely.

Das ist wunderbar (wundervoll).
That's wonderful.

Das ist vollkommen.
That's perfect.

Das ist verblüffend.
That's really something! Well, I never! It's
    stupendous!

Das gefällt mir.
I like that.

Das habe ich gern.
I like that.

2. I Don't Like It

Das ist nicht gut.
That's not good.

Das ist schlecht.
It's bad. That's bad.

Es ist nicht schön.
It's not nice (beautiful).

Das ist nicht schön von Ihnen.
That's not nice of you.

Das ist wertlos.
It's worthless.

Ich mag es nicht.
I don't like it.

Ich mag ihn nicht.
I don't like him.

Das gefällt mir nicht.
I don't like that. ("That doesn't please me.")

QUIZ 22

1. *Ich mag es nicht.*
2. *Das ist vollkommen.*
3. *Das ist schön.*
4. *Das ist verblüffend.*
5. *Das gefällt mir sehr.*
6. *Er ist sehr nett.*
7. *Das gefällt mir nicht.*
8. *Das ist schlecht.*
9. *Sie sind sehr liebenswürdig.*
10. *Das ist hervorragend.*

1. That's excellent. That's wonderful.
2. It's really something! Well, I never!
3. I'm very pleased with it.
4. He's very nice.
5. You're very kind.
6. That's bad.
7. That's beautiful.
8. I don't like that.
9. I don't like it.
10. That's perfect.

ANSWERS

1—9; 2—10; 3—7; 4—2; 5—3; 6—4; 7—8; 8—6; 9—5; 10—1.

EIN WITZ

Zwei Freunde gehen in ein Restaurant und jeder bestellt ein Beefsteak. Ein paar Minuten später kommt der Kellner zurück und bringt ein grosses und ein kleines Stück Fleisch. Der eine nimmt sich sofort das grosse Stuck. Der andere wird wütend und sagt zu ihm:

"Was für schlechte Manieren du hast! Weisst du nicht, dass du als erster das kleinere Stück hättest nehmen sollen?"

Der andere antwortet:
"Welches Stück hättest du denn genommen, wenn du an meiner Stelle wärest?"

"Das kleinere, natürlich," sagt der eine.

"Nun gut," antwortet der andere, "Worüber beschwerst du dich? Du hast es doch, nicht wahr?"

A JOKE

Two friends go to a restaurant and each orders a steak. A few minutes later the waiter comes back with a large piece of meat and a small one. One of the two immediately takes the large piece. The other is furious and says to him:

"What bad manners you have! Don't you know that since you were the first to help yourself you should have taken the smaller piece?"

The other answers:

"If you were in my place, which piece would you have taken?"

"The smaller one, of course," says the first one.

"Well, then," the other answers, "what are you complaining about? You have it, don't you?"

NOTES

1. *ein paar*—a few
   ein Paar—a pair

2. *Später kommt der Kellner zurück:* example of inversion.

3. *Werden* here is not used as an auxiliary but as the equivalent of "to become" in English.

4. *Ich hätte nehmen sollen:* pluperfect subjunctive.

   There is no *zu* before *nehmen*, because the auxiliary *sollen* rules the phrase.

5. *Du hättest genommen:* pluperfect subjunctive of *nehmen*

   wärest: imperfect subjunctive of *sein*—to be
   Note the use of the pluperfect and imperfect subjunctive in the contrary-to-fact statement.

6. *Worüber:* contraction of *über was.*

REVIEW QUIZ 3

1. *Er hat es* _____ (in) *seine Tasche getan.*
   a. *auf*
   b. *in*
   c. *unter*

2. *Es ist* _____ (under) *dem Stuhl.*
   a. *darin*
   b. *unter*
   c. *wenn*

3. *Sie können es* _____ (without) *Schwierigkeit tun.*
   a. *ohne*
   b. *durch*
   c. *wenn*

4. *Ich habe es* _____ (under) *einem Haufen*
   Papier gefunden.
   a. *über*
   b. *unter*
   c. *oben*

5. *Man sagt, es sei* _____ (true).
   a. *spricht*
   b. *wahr*
   c. *das*

6. *Ich* _____ (am going) *zur Bank.*
   a. *gehen*
   b. *geht*
   c. *gehe*

7. *Er* _____ (is going) *aufs Land.*
   a. *geht*
   b. *muss*
   c. *gehen*

8. *Geben Sie mir ein* _____ (little) *Wasser.*
   a. *wenig*
   b. *viel*
   c. *hier*

9. *Ich habe nicht* _____ (much) *Geld.*
   a. *wenig*
   b. *viel*
   c. *zu viel*

10. *Das ist* _____ (more) *als das.*
    a. *weniger*
    b. *mehr*
    c. *früh*

11. *Das ist nicht* _____ (enough).
    a. *noch*
    b. *gut*
    c. *genug*

12. *Sie ist* _____ (beautiful).
    a. *gut*
    b. *schön*
    c. *nett*

13. _____(as) *Sie wünschen.*
    a. *nicht*
    b. *wie*
    c. *sehr*

14. *Wir sind* _____ (all) *da.*
    a. *wie*
    b. *genug*
    c. *alle*

15. _____(all) *wissen es.*
    a. *Alle*
    b. *Sofort*
    c. *Ganz*

16. *Ich* _____ (think) *nicht.*
    a. *halten*
    b. *denke*
    c. *bin*

17. *Ich* _____ (hope) *nicht.*
    a. *besser*
    b. *hoffe*
    c. *nehme an*

18. *Das macht* _____ (nothing).
    a. *selbst*
    b. *nichts*
    c. *schon*

19. *Das ist* _____ (the same).
    a. *dasselbe*
    b. *schon*
    c. *natürlich*

20. *Sind Sie* _____ (already) *fertig?*
    a. selbst
    b. nichts
    c. schon

ANSWERS

1—b; 2—b; 3—a; 4—b; 5—b; 6—c; 7—a; 8—a; 9—b;
10—b; 11—c; 12—b; 13—b; 14—c; 15—a; 16—b;
17—b; 18—b; 19—a; 20—c.

WORD STUDY

studiéren	(to) study
Wurm (der)	worm
Kalb (das)	calf
Búlle (der)	bull
hart	hard
Wágen (der)	wagon
Mítte (die)	middle
Bündel (das)	bundle
Kartón (der)	carton
Farm (die)	farm

LESSON 31

(Who, What, Which, How, Why)

70. THE INTERROGATIVE PRONOUN

Wer?	Who?	
Was?	What?	Example: *Was hat er gesagt?*
		What did he say?

Wer is declined as follows:

wer	who	Example: *Wer hat das gesagt?*
		Who said that?

| *wessen* | whose | *Wessen Geld ist das?* |
| | | Whose money is that? |

| *wem* | to | *Wem haben Sie das gesagt?* |
| | whom | To whom did you say that? |

| *wen* | whom | *Wen lieben Sie?* |
| | | Whom do you love? |

1. Wer? Who?

Wer ist da?
Who is it?

Wer sind Sie?
Who are you?

Wer weiss das?
Who knows that?

Wer kommt mit uns?
Who's coming with us?

Wem gehört das?
Whose is it? (To whom does it belong?)

Für wen ist das?
Who's that for?

Mit wem sprechen Sie?
Whom are you talking to?

Über wen sprechen Sie?
Whom are you speaking about?

Mit wem kommen Sie?
Whom are you coming with?

Wen möchten Sie sehen?
Whom do you want to see?

Wen suchen Sie?
Whom are you looking for?

2. *Was?* What

Mit was?
With what?

Über was?
About what?

Wozu?
To what?

Was gibt es Neues?
What's new?

An wen denken Sie?
Whom are you thinking about?

Was brauchen Sie?
What do you need?

Was sagen Sie?
What are you saying?

Was sagen Sie dazu?
What do you say about that?

Was tun Sie?
What are you doing?

Was möchten Sie?
What do you want? What would you like?

Was wollen Sie jetzt tun?
What do you want to do now?

Was möchten Sie sagen?
What do you mean? What would you like to say?

Was suchen Sie?
What are you looking for?

Was haben Sie?
What do you have? What's the matter with you?
   What's wrong with you?

Was hat er?
What does he have? What's the matter with him?

These forms are used like nouns.

The masculine and feminine forms *Wer*, etc., refer only to persons.

The neuter form *Was* refers to things.

The masculine and feminine forms in the dative and accusative, *wem* and *wen*, do not change when preceded by a preposition.

Mit wem kommt er?	*Mit seinem Vater.*
With whom is he coming?	With his father.

Für wen kauft sie den Mantel?	*Für ihren Sohn.*
For whom is she buying the coat?	For her son.

However, the neuter form *Was* changes to *Wo* whenever connected with a preposition and it is contracted with that preposition.

Mit was	becomes	*womit*	With what?
Für was	becomes	*wofür*	For what
Zu was	becomes	*wozu*	To what?
Über was	becomes	*worüber*	About what?
Durch was	becomes	*wodurch*	By what?

Womit (mit was) sehen wir?—Mit den Augen.
With what do we see?—With our (the) eyes.

Wofür (für was) kämpfen sie?—Für die Freiheit.
What are they fighting for?—For (the) liberty.

3. *Welcher? Welche? Welches?*—Which (one)

These forms are used as adjectives or as nouns. They follow the same declension as the article *der, die, das.*

Welcher Garten ist der schönste?
Which garden is the most beautiful?

Welcher ist Ihr Garten?
Which one is your garden?

Welcher, welche, welches?
Which (one)?

Welcher Mann?
What man?

Welche Männer?
What men?

Welches Buch?
What book? Which book?

Welcher Tag ist heute?
What's today?

In welchem Monat sind wir?
What month is it? ("In which month are we?")

Welche Frau?
What woman?

Welche Frauen?
What women?

Welche Neuigkeiten?
What's new?

Welch ein Unterschied!
What a difference!

**Welcher Unterschied besteht zwischen den
    beiden Dingen?**
What's the difference between the two things?

4. *Was für ein, eine, ein?* What kind of?

Was für remains unchanged. *Ein, eine, ein* follows the declension of the indefinite article. In the plural *was für* stands without an article.

Was für ein Schuh ist das? Das ist ein schwarzer Schuh.
What kind of shoe is that? That is a black shoe.

Was für Schuhe sind das? Das sind schwarze Schuhe.
What kind of shoes are these? These are black shoes.

Das sind schwarze.
These are black ones.

Was für ein Mann?
What kind of man?

Was für Menschen?
What kind of people?

5. *Wie?* How?

Wie?
How?

Aber wie?
But how?

Wie meinen Sie das?
How's that? What do you mean?

Wie heissen Sie?
What's your name?

Wie heisst diese Stadt?
What is the name of this town?

Wie geht's?
How are you?

Wie schreibt man das Wort auf deutsch?
How do you write this word in German? How's
    this word written in German?

Wie sagen Sie das auf englisch?
How do you say that in English?

Wie sagen Sie "Thanks" auf deutsch?
How do you say "Thanks" in German?

Wie ist das geschehen?
How did that happen?

Wie macht man das?
How do you do that?

Wie haben Sie das gemacht?
How did you do (make) it?

Wie geht man dorthin?
How do you go there?

Wieviel Uhr ist es?
What's the time? ("What hour is it?")

Um wieviel Uhr?
What time? ("At what hour?")

6. *Wann?* When?

Wann ist das?
When is it?

Bis wann?
Until when?

Wann kommen Sie?
When are you coming?

Wann gehen Sie?
When are you leaving?

Wann kommt er?
When will he come? When is he coming?

Seit wann sind Sie hier?
How long have you been here?

7. *Warum?* Why?

Und warum nicht?
And why not?

Warum sagen Sie das?
Why do you say that?

Warum hat er das getan?
Why did he do it?

QUIZ 23

1. *Was tun Sie?*	1. What's new?
2. *Was wünschen Sie?*	2. What do you need?
3. *Was gibt es?*	3. And why not?
4. *Was möchten Sie sagen?*	4. Why do you say that?
5. *Was suchen Sie?*	5. Why did he do it?
6. *Wie heisst diese Strasse?*	6. What's your name?
7. *Was macht das aus?*	7. How are you?
8. *Welch ein Unterschied?*	8. But how?
9. *Welcher ist besser?*	9. When are you leaving?
10. *Wann fahren Sie ab?*	10. Who are you?
11. *Wer sind Sie?*	11. Whom do you want to see?
12. *Wen möchten Sie sehen?*	12. What a difference?
13. *Was brauchen Sie?*	13. Which is the better?

14. *Warum hat er es getan?*	14. What do you mean?
15. *Aber wie?*	15. What are you looking for?
16. *Wie geht's?*	16. What's the matter?
17. *Warum sagen Sie das?*	17. What difference does it make? What does it matter?
18. *Und warum nicht?*	18. What's the name of this street?
19. *Was gibt es Neues?*	19. What are you doing?
20. *Wie heissen Sie?*	20. What do you want?

ANSWERS

1—19; 2—20; 3—16; 4—14; 5—15; 6—18; 7—17;
8—12; 9—13; 10—9; 11—10; 12—11; 13—2; 14—5;
15—8; 16—7; 17—4; 18—3; 19—1; 20—6.

WORD STUDY

Komisch	comical
Muskel (der)	muscle
Fuss (der)	foot
Haar (das)	hair
Hand (die)	hand
Land (das)	land
Jüni (der)	June
Boot (das)	boat
Offizier (der)	officer
Insekt (das)	insect

71. HOW MUCH?

Der Preis?
The price?

Was ist der Preis?
What's the price? ("How is the price?")

Wieviel?
How much?

Wieviel macht es?
How much is it?

Wieviel für alles?
How much for everything? How much does it all cost?

Wieviel für jedes?
How much each?

Wieviel pro Dutzend?
How much a dozen?

Wieviel wollen Sie dafür haben?
How much do you want for it?

72. HOW MANY?

Wie viele?
How many?

Wieviel Geld?
How much (money)?

Wie viele Menschen?
How many people?

Wieviel Zeit?
How much time?

(Wieviel Zeit) bracht man, um dorthin zu kommen?
How long ("how much time") does it take to get there?

Wie viele sind dort?
How many are there?

Wie viele bleiben davon übrig?
How many of them are left?

Wie viele haben Sie davon?
How many of them ("of it") do you have?

Den wievielten haben wir heute?
What's (the date) today? ("How many have we today?")

Der wievielte ist Montag?
What's the date Monday? ("The how many will Monday be?")

QUIZ 24

1. *Wieviel gibt es davon?*
2. *Wieviel macht es?*
3. *Wieviel möchten Sie davon?*
4. *Welcher Preis?*
5. *Wieviel Zeit? Wie lange?*
6. *Den wievielten haben wir?*
7. *Wieviel bleibt davon übrig?*
8. *Wie viele haben Sie davon?*
9. *Welcher Preis ist das?*
10. *Der wievielte ist Montag?*

1. How much remains?
2. What's the date today? ("The how many?")
3. What's the date Monday?
4. What's the price?
5. What price?
6. How much is it?
7. How many do you want?
8. How much time? How long?
9. How many of them do you have?
10. How many are there?

ANSWERS

1—10; 2—6; 3—7; 4—5; 5—8; 6—2; 7—1; 8—9; 9—4; 10—3.

LESSON 32

(Useful Word Groups)

73. USEFUL WORD GROUPS

1. Some, Someone, Something, Sometimes

etwas
some, something

etwas Geld
some money

etwas Neues
Something new

Einige Menschen, einige Leute
some people

einige Wörter
some words, a few words

jemand
someone, somebody

Ist jemand hier, der das kann?
Is there anyone here who can do it?

manchmal
sometimes

Ich sehe ihn manchmal.
I see him sometimes.

2. Once, Twice

einmal
once, one time

zweimal
twice, two times

das erste Mal
the first time

das nächste Mal
the next time

das letzte Mal
the last time

noch einmal
another time; again; once more

jedes Mal, jedesmal
every time, each time

dieses Mal, diesmal
this time

3. Up to

bis
up to

bis jetzt
up to now

bis dort
up to there

bis zu Ende
(up) to the end

bis zum Bahnhof
up to (as far as) the station

bis heute abend
up to this evening
See you this evening.

bis morgen
up to tomorrow
See you tomorrow.

bis Montag
up to Monday
See you Monday.

4. I Need It

Ich brauche es.
I need it (that).

Das braucht er nicht.
He doesn't need it (that).

Brauchen Sie etwas?
Do you need anything?

Ich brauche nichts.
I don't need anything.

Ich brauche es überhaupt nicht.
I don't need it at all.

5. It's Necessary, I Must

Es ist unbedingt notwendig, dass ich Sie sehe.
It's absolutely necessary that I see you.

Sie müssen es ihm sagen.
You have to (must) tell him.

Sie müssen früh nach Hause kommen.
You must come home early.

Sie müssen die Wahrheit sagen.
You must tell the truth.

6. I Feel Like

Ich möchte es haben.
I'd like to have it. I feel like having it.

Ich möchte nicht dorthin gehen.
I don't feel like going there.

Ich möchte gern einen Apfel essen.
I feel like having an apple.

Möchten Sie gern den Film sehen?
Would you like to see this movie?

7. At the Home of

zu Hause
at home

bei
at the home of

Fühlen Sie sich wie zu Hause.
Make yourself at home.

Wir waren bei Freunden.
We were at some friends.

Ich werde Sie bei Müllers sehen.
I'll see you at the Müllers'.

Er war beim (bei dem) Schneider.
He was at the tailor's.

Kommen Sie zu uns.
Come over to our place.

als ich bei meinem Vater wohnte
when I was living with my father.

Ist Herr Müller zu Hause?
Is Mr. Müller at home?

Ich muss zum Arzt gehen.
I have to go to the doctor's.

8. Here It Is

Hier!
Here! Here it is!

Hier bin ich.
Here I am.

Hier ist er.
Here he is.

Hier ist sie.
Here she is.

Hier sind sie.
Here they are.

Hier ist das Buch.
Here's the book.

9. There It Is

Dort!
There it is!

Dort ist er.
There he is.

Dort ist sie.
There she is.

Dort sind sie.
There they are.

QUIZ 25

1. etwas Geld	1. to the end
2. einmal	2. I need that.
3. bis zu Ende	3. Here's the book.
4. Ich brauche das.	4. Some money.
5. Hier ist das Buch.	5. Once.

ANSWERS

1—4; 2—5; 3—1; 4—2; 5—3.

REVIEW QUIZ 4

1. _____ (What) *ist der Name dieser Stadt?*
   a. *Was*
   b. *Welches*
   c. *Wann*

2. _____ (Who) *sind Sie?*
   a. *Wer*
   b. *Welcher*
   c. *Was*

3. _____ (When) *wird er kommen?*
   a. *Wer*
   b. *Wann*
   c. *Welcher*

4. _____ (Why) *sagen Sie das?*
   a. *Einige*
   b. *Wann*
   c. *Warum*

5. *das* _____ (twelfth) *Kapitel*
   a. *zwölfte*
   b. *siebzehnte*
   c. *sechste*

6. *Der Hut hat mich* _____ (fifty-four) *Mark gekostet.*
   a. *zwei*
   b. *fünfzig*
   c. *vierundfünfzig*

7. *Ich wohne Nummer* _____ (seventeen) *Friedrichstrasse.*
   a. *dreiunddreissig*
   b. *siebzehn*
   c. *dreizehn*

8. *Es ist* _____ (noon).
   a. *Mittag*
   b. *Mitternacht*
   c. *elf Uhr*

9. *Wir sehen uns um* _____ (six) *Uhr.*
   a. *fünf*
   b. *sieben*
   c. *sechs*

10. *Es ist* _____ (time), *es zu tun.*
    a. *wieviel*
    b. *Zeit*
    c. *hier*

11. *Wir haben heute* _____ (Wednesday).
    a. *Dienstag*
    b. *Mittwoch*
    c. *Montag*

12. *Er fährt* _____ (Tuesday) *ab.*
    a. *Dienstag*
    b. *Juli*
    c. *August*

13. *Heute ist der erste _____* (June).
   a. *Juni*
   b. *Juli*
   c. *August*

14. *Er _____* (need) *das nicht.*
   a. *das*
   b. *braucht*
   c. *alles*

15. *_____* (how) *schreibt man das Wort auf deutsch?*
   a. *Warum*
   b. *Wie*
   c. *Dieses*

16. *Ich bin am _____* (twelve) *April geboren.*
   a. *Mai*
   b. *elften*
   c. *zwölften*

17. *_____* (Here's) *das Buch.*
   a. *Hier ist*
   b. *Dort ist*
   c. *Wir*

18. *Ich habe mein _____* (money) *verloren.*
   a. *Kabine*
   b. *Geld*
   c. *Hof*

19. *Er arbeitet von _____* (morning) *bis abends.*
   a. *morgens*
   b. *nachts*
   c. *Tag*

20. *An welcher Station muss ich _____* (get off)?
   a. *sind*
   b. *aussteigen*
   c. *noch*

ANSWERS

1—a; 2—a; 3—b; 4—c; 5—a; 6—c; 7—b; 8—a; 9—c;
10—b; 11—b; 12—a; 13—a; 14—b; 15—b; 16—c;
17—a; 18—b; 19—a; 20—b.

WORD STUDY

Parfüm (das)	perfume
falsch	false
freundlich	friendly
frisch	fresh
grün	green
neu	new
Austrálien (das)	Australia
rund	round
März	March
bréchen	(to) break

LESSON 33

(Getting Around)

74. GETTING AROUND

Verzeihung.
Pardon me.

Entschuldigen Sie.
Excuse me.

Wie heisst diese Stadt?
What is the name of this town?

Wie weit sind wir von Berlin?
How far are we from Berlin?

Wie viele Kilometer sind es von hier bis Berlin?
How many kilometers from here to Berlin?

Von hier sind es zehn Kilometer.
It's ten kilometers from here.

Das ist zwanzig Kilometer von hier.
That's twenty kilometers from here.

Wie komme ich von hier nach Berlin?
How do I get to Berlin from here?

Fahren Sie diese Strasse entlang.
Follow this road.

Können Sie mir sagen, wie ich zu dieser Adresse komme?
Can you tell me how I can get to this address?

Können Sie mir sagen, wie ich nach diesem Ort komme?
Can you tell me how I can get to this place?

Wie heisst diese Strasse?
What is the name of this street?

Können Sie mir sagen, wo sich diese Strasse befindet?
Can you tell me where this street is?

Wo ist die Kaiserstrasse?
Where is Kaiser Street?

Ist es weit von hier?
Is it far from here?

Ist es in der Nähe?
Is it near here?

Es ist der dritte Block rechts.
It's the third block to the right.

Gehen Sie diesen Weg.
Go this way.

Gehne Sie geradeaus.
Go straight ahead.

Gehen Sie bis zur Ecke und dann links.
Go to the corner and turn left.

Nehmen Sie die erste Seitenstrasse rechts.
Turn right ("Take the first side street to the right").

Wo befindet sich die Garage?
Where is the garage?

Wo befindet sich das Polizeiamt?
Where is the police station?

Wo befindet sich das Rathaus?
Where is the City Hall?

Wo ist die Omnibushaltestelle?
Where is the bus stop?

An welcher Station muss ich aussteigen?
What station do I get off at?

Wo muss ich aussteigen?
Where do I get off?

Wo ist der Bahnhof?
Where is the railroad station?

Wo bekomme ich den Zug nach Berlin?
Where do I get the train for Berlin?

Auf Gleis zwei.
On track two.

Der Zug ist gerade abgefahren.
The train just left.

LESSON 34

(Writing, Phoning, Telegraphing)

75. WRITING, PHONING, TELEGRAPHING

Um wieviel Uhr fährt der nächste Zug ab?
What time does the next train leave?

Kann ich eine Rückfahrkarte nach Berlin haben?
May I have a round-trip ticket for Berlin?

Wieviel macht das?
How much is that?

Fünfzig Mark und fünfundzwanzig Pfennige.
Fifty marks and twenty-five pfennigs.

Wie lange dauert die Reise?
How long does it take to get there (''does the trip last'')?

Etwas über eine Stunde.
A little over an hour.

Ich möchte einen Brief schreiben.
I'd like to write a letter.

Haben Sie einen Bleistift?
Have you a pencil?

Haben Sie eine Feder?
Do you have a pen?

Haben Sie Löschpapier?
Do you have a blotter.

Haben Sie einen Briefumschlag?
Do you have an envelope?

Haben Sie eine Briefmarke?
Do you have a stamp?

Wo kann ich eine Briefmarke kaufen?
Where can I buy a stamp?

Haben Sie eine Luftpostmarke?
Do you have an air-mail stamp?

Wo befindet sich das Postamt?
Where is the post office?

Ich möchte diesen Brief aufgeben.
I'd like to mail this letter.

Wie viele Briefmarken brauche ich für diesen Brief?
How many stamps do I need on this letter?

Wo ist der Briefkasten?
Where is the mailbox?

An der Ecke.
At the corner.

Ich möchte ein Telegramm senden.
I'd like to send a telegram.

Wo kann ich ein Telegramm aufgeben?
Where can I send a telegram?

Wo befindet sich das Telegrafenamt?
Where is the telegraph office?

Es ist im Postamt.
It's in the post office.

Wieviel kostet ein Telegramm nach Berlin?
How much is a telegram to Berlin?

Wie lange läuft es dorthin?
How long will it take to get there?

Gibt es ein Telefon hier?
Is there a phone here?

Wo kann ich telefonieren?
Where can I phone?

Wo befindet sich das Telefon?
Where is the telephone?

Wo ist ein öffentlicher Fernsprecher?
Where is the phone booth?

Im Zigarengeschäft.
In the tobacco shop.

LESSON 35

(Family Affairs I)

Darf ich lhr Telefon benutzen?
May I use your phone?

Selbstverständlich! Bitte sehr!
Of course! Go ahead!

Fräulein, ein Ferngespräch, bitte.
May I have long distance, please?

Was kostet ein Gespräch nach Berlin?
How much is a (telephone) call to Berlin?

**Fräulein, bitte MITTE sieben elf
einundzwanzig.**
MITTE 7 11 21, please, operator.

Einen Augenblick, bitte.
One moment, please.

Die Leitung ist besetzt.
The line's busy.

Fräulein, Sie haben mich falsch verbunden.
Operator, you gave me the wrong number.

Niemand antwortet.
There is no answer.

Kann ich bitte Herr Wagner sprechen?
May I speak to Mr. Wagner, please?

Am Apparat.
Speaking.

Hier Lorenz.
This is Mr. Lorenz speaking.

76. FAMILY AFFAIRS

Wie heissen Sie?
What is your name?

Ich heisse Hans Bauer.
My name is Hans Bauer.

Wie heisst er?
What is his name?

Er heisst Fritz Müller.
His name is Fritz Müller.

Wie heisst sie?
What is her name?

Sie heisst Lotte Schneider.
Her name is Lotte Schneider.

Wie heissen sie?
What are their names?

Er heisst Ludwig Schmitz und sie heisst Grete Meier.
His name is Ludwig Schmitz and hers is Grete Meier.

Was ist sein Vorname?
What's his first name?

Sein Vorname ist Karl.
His first name is Karl.

Was ist sein Familienname?
What is his last name?

Sein Familienname ist Meier.
His last name is Meier.

Woher sind Sie?
Where are you from?

Ich komme aus Berlin.
I'm from Berlin.

Wo sind Sie geboren?
Where were you born?

Ich bin in Hamburg geboren.
I was born in Hamburg.

LESSON 36

(Family Affairs II)

Wie alt sind Sie?
How old are you?

Ich bin zwanzig Jahre alt.
I'm twenty (years old).

Ich werde einundzwanzig im September.
I'll be twenty-one in September.

**Ich wurde am neunzehnten August
  neunzehnhundertfünfunddreissig geboren.**
I was born August 19, 1935.

Wie viele Brüder haben Sie?
How many brothers do you have?

Ich habe zwei Brüder.
I have two brothers.

Der älteste ist zweiundzwanzig.
The oldest is twenty-two.

Er besucht die Universität.
He attends the university.

Der jüngste ist siebzehn.
The youngest is seventeen.

Er ist das letzte Jahr auf dem Gymnasium.
He's in the last year of the "Gymnasium" (college
  prep school).

Wie viele Schwestern haben Sie?
How many sisters do you have?

Ich habe eine Schwester.
I have one sister.

Sie ist fünfzehn.
She's fifteen.

Was tut Ihr Vater?
What does your father do?

Er ist Rechtsanwalt.
He's a lawyer.

Er ist Architekt.
He's an architect.

Er ist Lehrer.
He's a teacher.

Er ist Universitätsprofessor.
He's a university professor.

Er ist Arzt.
He's a doctor.

Er ist Geschäftsmann.
He's in business.

Er ist im Textilhandel.
He's in the textile business.

Er ist Landwirt.
He's a farmer.

Er ist Beamter.
He's a government employee.

Er ist Arbeiter.
He's a worker.

Er arbeitet in einer Automobilfabrik.
He works in an automobile factory.

Wann ist Ihr Geburtstag?
When is your birthday?

Mein Geburtstag ist in swei Wochen, am dreiundzwanzigsten Januar.
My birthday is in two weeks, January 23rd.

Haben Sie Verwandte hier?
Do you have any relatives here?

Wohnt Ihre ganze Familie hier?
Does your whole family live here?

Meine ganze Familie ausser meinen Grosseltern.
All my family except my grandparents.

Sie wohnen auf einem Gut, in Westfalen.
They live in a country home, in Westphalia.

Sind Sie mit Herr Schneider verwandt?
Are you related to Mr. Schneider?

Er ist mein Onkel.
He's my uncle.

Er ist mein Vetter.
He's my cousin.

Sind Sie mit Frau Müller verwandt?
Are you related to Mrs. Müller?

Sie ist meine Tante.
She's my aunt.

Sie ist meine Kusine.
She's my cousin.

REVIEW QUIZ 5

1. *Wie heisst* _____ (this) *Stadt?*
   a. *dieser*
   b. *dieses*
   c. *diese*

2. _____ (how) *komme ich von hier nach Berlin?*
   a. *Wieviel*
   b. *Wie*
   c. *Welcher*

3. _____ (How) *heisst diese Strasse?*
   a. *Was*
   b. *Wann*
   c. *Wie*

4. _____ (Where) *ist die Friedrichstrasse?*
   a. *Wo*
   b. *Wann*
   c. *Dass*

5. _____ (go) *diesen Weg?*
   a. *Gehen Sie*
   b. *Gehen*
   c. *Gehen sie*

6. *Gehen Sie zur Ecke und nehmen Sie die erste*
   _____ (left).
   a. *links*
   b. *rechts*
   c. *weit*

7. _____ (How much) *macht es?*
   a. *Wie*
   b. *Wieviel*
   c. *Dass*

8. *Ich möchte einen Brief* _____ (to write).
   a. *schreiben Sie*
   b. *schreiben*
   c. *schreibe*

9. *Wo kann ich eine* _____ (stamp) *kaufen?*
    a. *Briefmarke*
    b. *Post*
    c. *Stempel*

10. *An der Ecke von dieser* _____ (street).
    a. *Strasse*
    b. *hier*
    c. *Allee*

11. _____ (Is there) *ein Telefon hier?*
    a. *Gibt es*
    b. *Es gibt*
    c. *Das*

12. *Fräulein, Sie haben mich* _____ (wrong) *verbunden.*
    a. *falsch*
    b. *viel*
    c. *nicht*

13. *Was ist sein* _____ (first name)?
    a. *Vorname*
    b. *Familie*
    c. *nennt sich*

14. *Wo sind Sie* _____ (born)?
    a. *gewesen*
    b. *geboren*
    c. *gekommen*

15. *Der jüngste ist siebzehn* _____ (years) *alt.*
    a. *Jahre*
    b. *Jahr*
    c. *jährlich*

16. *Er ist* _____ (lawyer).
    a. *Professor*
    b. *Rechtsanwalt*
    c. *Beamter*

17. *Er ist* _____ (worker).
    a. *Arbeiter*
    b. *arbeitet*
    c. *Fabrik*

18. *Sie wohnen auf einem Gut*, _____ (near)
    von Westfalen.
    a. *in der Nähe*
    b. *sehr*
    c. *weit*

19. _____ (follow) *dieser Strassenbahn.*
    a. *Gehen Sie*
    b. *Folgen Sie*
    c. *Nehmen Sie*

20. *Ist es* _____ (far) *von hier?*
    a. *weit*
    b. *Ecke*
    c. *nahe*

21. *Auf* _____ (track) *zwei.*
    a. *Gleis*
    b. *Rückkehr*
    c. *Zug*

22. *Das bin* _____ (I).
    a. *ich*
    b. *mir*
    c. *mich*

23. *Das ist nicht* _____ (free).
    a. *frei*
    b. *früh*
    c. *falsch*

24. *Sind Sie* _____ (related) *mit Herr Schneider?*
    a. *verwandt*
    b. *Bruder*
    c. *Familie*

25. *Meine ganze Familie* _____ (except) *meinen
    Grosseltern.*
    a. *ausser*
    b. *auf*
    c. *davon*

ANSWERS

1—c; 2—b; 3—c; 4—a; 5—a; 6—a; 7—b; 8—b; 9—a;
10—a; 11—a; 12—a; 13—a; 14—b; 15—a; 16—b;
17—a; 18—a; 19—b; 20—a; 21—a; 22—a; 23—a;
24—a; 25—a.

LESSON 37

(Shopping)

77. SHOPPING

Einkäufe
purchases

1. **Wieviel kostet es?**
   How much is it?

2. **Zehn Mark.**
   Ten marks.

3. **Das ist zu teuer. Haben Sie nichts anderes?**
   That's too expensive. Haven't you anything else?

4. **Von derselben Sorte?**
   Of the same kind?

5. **Ja, dasselbe oder etwas ähnliches.**
   Yes, the same kind or something similar.

6. **Wir haben so etwas.**
   We have this.

7. **Können Sie mir nichts anderes zeigen?**
   Don't you have anything else to show me?

8. **Etwas billigeres?**
   Something cheaper?

9. **Wenn möglich.**
If possible.

10. **Möchten Sie so etwas?**
Would you like this?

11. **Das kommt auf den Preis an.**
That depends on the price.

12. **Das kostet acht Mark.**
This is eight marks.

13. **Und das hier? Ist es billiger oder teurer?**
How about this? Is it cheaper or more expensive?

14. **Teurer.**
More expensive.

15. **Haben Sie nichts anderes?**
Haven't you anything else?

16. **Im Moment nicht, aber ich erwarte einige Neuheiten.**
Not at the moment, but I'm expecting some new styles.

17. **Wann?**
When?

18. **Jeden Tag. Kommen Sie gegen Ende der Woche.**
Any day now. Drop in toward the end of the week.

19. **Ganz bestimmt. Übrigens, wieviel kostet es?**
I'll do that. By the way, how much is this?

20. **Zwei Mark das Paar.**
Two marks a pair.

21. **Geben Sie mir ein Dutzend.**
Let me have a dozen.

22. **Möchten Sie sie mitnehmen?**
Will you take them with you?

23. **Nein, bitte lassen Sie sie mir schicken.**
No, please have them delivered.

24. **Immer noch an dieselbe Adresse?**
Still at the same address?

25. **Ja, es ist immer noch dieselbe.**
Yes, it's still the same.

26. **Danke schön. Auf Wiedersehen.**
Thank you very much. Good-by.

27. **Auf Wiedersehen.**
Good-by.

NOTES

1. *Wieviel kostet es?* How much does it cost? *Was macht es?* How much does that make?

4. *Von:* always with the dative case.

5. *Ähnliches* has neuter declension, because it refers to *etwas* which is always neuter.

6. *So etwas:* Something like this.

8. *Etwas billigeres:* Something cheaper; neuter declension.

10. *Möchten sie:* Would you like to?; polite form to express a want or wish; (conditional of *mögen*)

11. *ankommen (an-kommen):* separable prefix idiomatically, to depend on.

12. *Mark:* always singular.

13. Comparative: two examples of the comparative. Note that the second *e* in *teuer* is dropped in the comparative form.

16. *Im:* contraction of *in dem* (dative). *Einige:* Use for *etwas* to express something precise.

18. *Jeden Tag:* accusative as generally used for expressions of time. *Gegen Ende* (idiomatic) toward the end; requires no article.

19. *Ganz bestimmt:* "Quite definite."
21. *mir:* Dative of the personal pronoun.
22. *Mitnehmen (mit-nehmen):* separable prefix. *Ich nahm es mit.* I took it along.
23. *Schicken lassen:* to have something sent. *machen lassen:* to have something done or made; *bauen lassen:* to have something built; etc.
24. *an* plus accusative (motion toward a destination).

QUIZ 26

1. _____ (How much) *macht das?*
   a. Wieviel
   b. Wie
   c. Wann

2. *Von derselben* _____ (kind).
   a. Sorte
   b. Sache
   c. teuer

3. *Ja, von derselben Sorte* _____ (or) *etwas ähnliches.*
   a. wann
   b. oder
   c. und

4. *Es gibt* _____ (this).
   a. den
   b. das
   c. dieser

5. *Etwas* _____ (less).
   a. aber
   b. weniger
   c. nichts

6. _____ (that) *kommt auf den Preis an.*
   a. Das
   b. Dieses
   c. Dem

7. *Nicht im Moment,* _____ (but) *ich erwarte*
Neuheiten.
   a. oder
   b. aber
   c. das

8. _____ (When) *denn?*
   a. Wie
   b. Wieviel
   c. Wann

9. *Geben Sie mir ein Dutzend* _____ (of them).
   a. dort
   b. davon
   c. dann

10. *Nein, schicken Sie* _____ (them) *mir, bitte.*
   a. sie
   b. ihnen
   c. es

ANSWERS

1—a; 2—a; 3—b; 4—c; 5—b; 6—a; 7—b; 8—c; 9—b;
10—a.

78. ORDERING BREAKFAST

Das Frühstück
Breakfast

1. **M.: Du bist sicher hungrig?**
   M.: You must be hungry. ("You are certainly
   hungry.")

2. **Frau M.: Ja, ich könnte wirklich etwas essen.**
   Mrs. M.: Yes, I could certainly eat something.

3. **G.: Es gibt ein gutes Restaurant im Hotel.**
   G.: There's a good restaurant at the hotel.

4. **Frau M.: Das ist eine gute Idee, gehen wir.**
   Mrs. M.: That's a good idea. Let's go.

5. **M.: Ober! Ober!**
   M.: Waiter!

6. **W.: Bitte sehr, meine Herrschaften?**
   W.: Yes ("sirs")?

7. **M.: Das Frühstück, bitte!**
   M.: We'd like breakfast.

8. **Frau M.: Was gibt es?**
   Mrs. M.: What do you have?

9. **W.: Kaffee, Tee mit Zitrone oder Sahne,
   oder auch Schokolade.**
   W.: Coffee, tea with lemon or cream, or else
   (hot) chocolate.

10. **Frau M.: Und was noch?**
    Mrs. M.: What else?

11. **W.: Brötchen oder Brot.**
    W.: Rolls or bread.

12. **Frau M.: Keine Butter?**
    Mrs. M.: No butter?

13. **W.: Sicher, gnädige Frau, Butter und Mar-
    melade.**
    W.: Of course, madam, butter and jelly.

14. **Frau M.: Ich möchte Kaffee und Brötchen.**
    Mrs. M.: I'd like some coffee and rolls.

15. **M.: Geben Sie mir dasselbe und auch ein Ei.**
    M.: Let me have the same and an egg as well.

16. **W.: Gewiss, mein Herr. Möchten Sie sonst
    noch etwas?**
    W.: Certainly, sir. Would you like anything
    else?

17. **M.: Nein, das ist alles.**
    M.: No, that'll be all.

18. **Frau M.: Herr Ober, eine Serviette, bitte.**
    Mrs. M.: Waiter, may I have a napkin, please?

19. **M.: Würden Sie mir auch eine Gabel
    bringen?**
    Can you also let me have a fork?

20. **Frau M.: Auch etwas mehr Zucker, bitte.**
    Mrs. M.: And some more sugar, please.

21. **W.: Bitte sehr, gnädige Frau.**
    W.: Here you are, Madam.

22. **Frau M.: Mein Kaffee ist kalt. Bitte, bringen Sie mir eine andere Tasse.**
    Mrs. M.: My coffee is cold. Please bring me another cup.

23. **W.: Gern.**
    W.: Gladly.

24. **M.: Ober, die Rechnung bitte.**
    M.: Waiter, may I have the check?

25. **W.: Hier bitte, mein Herr.**
    W.: Here you are, sir.

26. **M.: Hier, behalten Sie das Kleingeld!**
    M.: Here, keep the change.

27. **W.: Danke schön, mein Herr. Auf Wiedersehen, gnädige Frau.**
    W.: Thank you very much, sir. Good-by, Madam.

28. **M.: Auf Wiedersehen.**
    M.: Good-by.

NOTES

2. *Könnte:* subjunctive of *können. Essen* without *zu* because it comes after *können.*

3. *Ein gutes Restaurant:* observe the declension of the adjective with *ein;* (singular, accusative).

4. *Eine gute Idee:* (nominative, feminine, singular).

5. *Ober:* abbreviation of *Oberkellner;* also *Herr Ober.*

6. The expression *bitte* "please" here corresponds to the English "What can I do for you?" *Bitte* is also often used to reinforce the polite idea in a request or statement.

7. *Das Frühstück:* breakfast
   Das Mittagessen: lunch
   Das Abendessen: dinner

8. *Was gibt es?:* What is there?
11. *Brötchen* is the diminutive of *Brot*, "bread";
    therefore: "little bread." Words ending in *-chen*
    or *-lein* indicate a diminutive. (They are always
    neuter.):
    Kätzchen: kitty
    Fräulein: young lady
12. *Butter* Some butter; *Keine Butter* no butter.
13. *Gnädige Frau*—gracious lady; a polite way to
    address a lady in German.
15. *Ein Ei:* an egg; *Gekochte Eier:* Boiled eggs
    Eier: eggs; *Spiegeleier:* fried eggs; (sunny side
    up) *Rühreier:* scrambled eggs
16. *Sonst noch etwas?* Anything else? ("Apart from
    that, something else?")
21. *Bitte:* Here you are. (Another polite form of
    bitte)
23. *Mit Vergnügen:* with pleasure
26. *Kleingeld:* change ("small money")

79. A SAMPLE MENU

Speisenfolge	Menu
Frühlingssuppe	Vegetable soup
Schinkenomelette	Ham omelet
Gebackenes Hünchen	Roast chicken
Grüne Prinzessbohnen	String beans
Salzkartoffeln	Boiled potatoes
Salat	Salad
Käseplatte	Assorted cheeses
Gebäck	Pastry
Kaffee und Liköre	Coffee and Liqueurs

REVIEW QUIZ 6

1. *Du musst Hunger* _____ (have).
   a. *sein*
   b. *haben*
   c. *gut*

2. *Keine* _____ (butter).
   a. *Bier*
   b. *Butter*
   c. *Brot*

3. _____ (There is) *ein gutes Restaurant im Hotel.*
   a. *Es gibt*
   b. *Gibt es*
   c. *Das ist*

4. *Mein Kaffee ist* _____ (cold).
   a. *kalt*
   b. *warm*
   c. *Sache*

5. *Geben Sie mir* _____ (the same).
   a. *auch*
   b. *dasselbe*
   c. *Butter*

6. *Ober, eine* _____ (napkin) *bitte!*
   a. *Gabel*
   b. *Messer*
   c. *Serviette*

7. *Würden Sie mir* _____ (also) *eine Gabel geben?*
   a. *sehr*
   b. *nicht*
   c. *auch*

8. *Ober,* _____ (the check).
   a. *einmal*
   b. *der Ober*
   c. *die Rechnung*

9. *Etwas* _____ (more) *Zucker.*
   a. *gefällt*
   b. *mir*
   c. *mehr*

10. *Behalten Sie das* _____ (change).
   a. *viel*
   b. *Kleingeld*
   c. *lassen*

ANSWERS

1—b; 2—b; 3—a; 4—a; 5—b; 6—c; 7—c; 8—c; 9—c;
10—b.

LESSON 38

▭▭ ▭▭

(Apartment Hunting)

80. APARTMENT HUNTING

1. **Ich komme wegen der Wohnung.**
   I've come about the apartment.

2. **Welche, bitte?**
   Which one, please?

3. **Die, zu vermieten ist.**
   The one for rent.

4. **Aber es gibt zwei.**
   But there are two.

5. **Können Sie mir eine Beschreibung geben?**
   Can you describe them?

6. **Die im fünften Stock ist unmöbliert.**
   The one on the fifth floor is unfurnished.

7. **Und die andere?**
   And the other?

8. **Die auf der zweiten Etage ist möbliert.**
   The one on the second floor is furnished.

9. **Wieviele Zimmer hat jede?**
   How many rooms does each one have?

10. **Die auf der fünften Etage hat vier Zimmer, Küche und Bad.**
The one on the fifth floor has four rooms, a kitchen and bath.

11. **Liegt sie nach dem Hof hinaus?**
Does it face the court?

12. **Nein, nach der Strasse.**
No, the street.

13. **Und die im zweiten Stock?**
And how about the one on the second floor?

14. **Sie hat fünf Zimmer, drei Schlafzimmer, ein Esszimmer und ein Wohnzimmer.**
It has five rooms, three bedrooms, a dining room and a parlor.

15. **Liegt sie auch nach dem Hof hinaus?**
Is it also on the court?

16. **Nein, auch nach der Strasse.**
No, it faces the street.

17. **Wie hoch ist die Miete?**
What's the rent?

18. **Die grössere kostet dreihundert Mark ohne Gas, Wasser und Strom.**
The larger one is three hundred marks without gas, water and electricity.

19. **Und die möblierte Wohnung?**
And the furnished apartment?

20. **Vierhundert Mark.**
That's four-hundred marks.

21. **Was für Möbel hat sie? Und in welchem Zustand sind sie?**
What kind of furniture does it have? And is it in good condition?

22. **Es sind antike Möbel in bestem Zustand.**
It's antique furniture (and) in excellent condition.

23. **Sind Wäsche und Silber einbegriffen?**
Are linens and silverware included?

24. **Sie finden alles, was man braucht, sogar eine vollständige Kücheneinrichtung.**
You'll find everything you need, even a complete set of kitchen utensils.

25. **Würde der Besitzer einen Mietvertrag mit mir machen? Und auf wie lange?**
Would the owner give me a lease? And for how long?

26. **Deswegen müssen Sich sich an den Hausverwalter wenden.**
You'd have to see the renting agent for that.

27. **Wie sind die Bedingungen?**
What are the terms?

28. **Sie zahlen drei Monate im voraus.**
You pay three months' rent in advance.

29. **Sonst nichts?**
Nothing else?

30. **Referenzen, selbstverständlich.**
References, of course.

31. **Übrigens, ist ein Fahrstuhl vorhanden?**
By the way, is there an elevator?

32. **Nein, es ist keiner da.**
No, there isn't.

33. **Das ist schade.**
That's too bad.

34. **Davon abgesehen, ist das Haus aber ganz modern.**
Apart from that, though, the house is quite modern.

35. **Wie meinen Sie das?**
What do you mean?

36. **Es hat Zentralheizung und eine Hintertreppe.**
There's central heating and a back stairway.

37. **Ist fliessendes Wasser vorhanden, warm und kalt?**

Is there hot and cold running water?

38. **Natürlich. Die Badezimmer wurden kürzlich renoviert.**

Of course. The bathrooms were remodeled recently.

39. **Sind eingebaute Schränke vorhanden?**

Are there any closets?

40. **Ja, einige grosse.**

Yes, several large ones.

41. **Ich vergass; sind Dienstbotenzimmer da?**

I forgot; are there servants' quarters?

42. **Ja, sie sind auch heizbar und haben elektrisches Licht.**

Yes, they are also heated and have electricity.

43. **Kann man sie sehen?**

When can I see them? (Can one see them?)

44. **Nur am Morgen.**

Only in the morning.

45. **Sehr gut. Ich werde morgen früh kommen. Besten Dank.**

Very well, I'll come tomorrow morning. Thanks a lot.

46. **Keine Ursache, gern zu Ihren Diensten.**

Not at all, glad to be of service.

NOTES

1. *Wegen:* because of (another preposition with the genitive.)
3. *Die, welche:* "The one which" Observe the comma after the relative pronoun *die*.
5. *Können Sie mir eine Beschreibung geben?*—Can you give me a description?
6. *Die:* "the one"
   Auf der: (Dative)

In Germany the first floor is *das Erdgeschoss* ("Ground floor").

Therefore the first floor, *erster Stock,* is really the second floor for us.

9. *Jede* (standing alone) is "each one" and can also be used with a noun:
   jeder Mann—"each or every man"
   Here *jede* is feminine because it refers to the apartment: *die Wohnung.*

11. *Liegt sie nach dem Hof?*—Does it lie toward the court?
    nach is always followed by the dative.

14. *Schlafzimmer:* bedroom ("sleeping room")
    Esszimmer: dining room ("eating room")
    Wohnzimmer: living room or parlor.

17. *Wie hoch ist die Miete?*—How high is the rent?
    Die Miete: the rent
    mieten: to rent

22. *Die Möbel:* furniture
    Das Möbel: a piece of furniture

23. *Die Wäsche:* linen; *also* laundry (underwear, etc.)
    Die Wäscherei: laundry (a place)

24. *Was man braucht:* "What one needs" *man* is used much more frequently than the English "one"

37. Notice that *fliessendes* placed before the neuter noun *Wasser* is declined, whereas *warm* and *kalt,* used alone, are not.

41. *Ich vergass:* I forgot; Imperfect of *vergessen* (strong verb); see No. 85.
    Das Dienstbotenzimmer: a compound noun, typical of German ("Room for the servants")

44. *Am Morgen: (an dem Morgen)*

45. *Ich werde kommen:* Future of *kommen,* to come (see No. 85.)

46. *Keine Ursache*—("no cause, no reason") *Gern zu Ihren Diensten.*—("Gladly at your service.")

QUIZ 27

1. _____ (How many) *Zimmer haben Sie?*
   a. *Anderes*
   b. *Wieviele*
   c. *Jede*

2. *Liegen sie nach der* _____ (street)?
   a. *Hof*
   b. *Salon*
   c. *Strasse*

3. *Was ist der* _____ (price)?
   a. *Preis*
   b. *tausend*
   c. *Art*

4. *Man* _____ (pays) *drei Monate im voraus.*
   a. *sind*
   b. *verstanden*
   c. *zahlt*

5. *Das* _____ (house) *ist sehr modern.*
   a. *Halle*
   b. *Haus*
   c. *Bad*

6. *Es ist fliessendes Wasser vorhanden* _____ (warm) *und kalt.*
   a. *warm*
   b. *schmutzig*
   c. *warmer*

7. *Sind* _____ (rooms) *für Dienstboten vorhanden?*
   a. *zahlreich*
   b. *Zimmer*
   c. *Flur*

8. _____ (Only) *morgens.*
   a. *Besuchen*
   b. *Nur*
   c. *Geheizt*
9. *Ich komme* _____ (tomorrow) *früh.*
   a. *morgen*
   b. *nur*
   c. *sehr*
10. _____ (Thank you) *vielmals.*
   a. *Morgen*
   b. *Dienst*
   c. *Danke*

ANSWERS

1—b; 2—c; 3—a; 4—c; 5—b; 6—a; 7—b; 8—b; 9—a;
10—c.

REVIEW QUIZ 7

1. *Ich ziehe* _____ (that you) *vor.*
   a. *das*
   b. *dieses*
   c. *die*
2. *Was soll* _____ (this) *heissen?*
   a. *das*
   b. *dort*
   c. *dieser*
3. *Ich weiss nicht* _____ (how).
   a. *noch*
   b. *oft*
   c. *wie*
4. *Er kommt* _____ (never).
   a. *wenn*
   b. *nie*
   c. *wie*
5. *Er hat* _____ (nothing) *gesagt.*
   a. *mehr*
   b. *wann*
   c. *nichts*

6. *Ihr Buch ist besser als* _____ (his) *Buch.*
   a. *Ihr*
   b. *sein*
   c. *mein*

7. *Ich bin* _____ (happy), *Sie kennenzulernen.*
   a. *erfreut*
   b. *vorstellen*
   c. *Bekanntschaft*

8. *Bis zur nächsten* _____ (week).
   a. *wahr*
   b. *Woche*
   c. *mal*

9. *Bis zum* _____ (next) *Mal.*
   a. *neulich*
   b. *nächsten*
   c. *Tage*

10. *Es geht gut,* _____ (thanks).
    a. *denke*
    b. *danke*
    c. *wie*

11. *Rufen Sie mich dieser* _____ (days) *an.*
    a. *Woche*
    b. *Tage*
    c. *neu*

12. _____ (Know) *Sie meinen Freund?*
    a. *Kennen*
    b. *Treffen*
    c. *Denke*

13. *Nein, ich* _____ (think) *nicht.*
    a. *Vergnügen*
    b. *denke*
    c. *kenne*

14. *Ich* _____ (hope), *Sie bald wiederzusehen.*
    a. *erfreut*
    b. *gemacht*
    c. *hoffe*

15. *Ich werde es Ihnen* _____ (write).
   a. *gehabt*
   b. *schreiben*
   c. *wiederfinden*
16. *Sie können mich* _____ (in the morning)
   anrufen.
   a. *Nummer*
   b. *Adresse*
   c. *morgens*
17. *Ich habe ihn* _____ (met).
   a. *erfreut*
   b. *getroffen*
   c. *rufen*
18. _____ (give) *Sie mir Ihre Adresse.*
   a. *Gehen*
   b. *Geben*
   c. *Rufen*
19. *Das ist sehr* _____ (good).
   a. *gut*
   b. *bald*
   c. *ganz*
20. *Auf* _____ (soon).
   a. *bald*
   b. *morgen*
   c. *auch*

ANSWERS

1—b; 2—a; 3—c; 4—b; 5—c; 6—b; 7—a; 8—b; 9—b;
10—b; 11—b; 12—a; 13—b; 14—c; 15—b; 16—c;
17—b; 18—b; 19—a; 20—a.

LESSON 39

(To Come, To Say, To Do)

81. TO COME, TO SAY, TO DO

1. *kommen* to come

ich komme	I come	*ihr kommt*	you come
wir kommen	we come	*Sie kommen*	you come
du kommst	you come	*sie kommen*	they come
er kommt	he comes		

Komm!	Come! (*fam.*)
Kommen Sie!	Come! (*pol.*)
Kommen Sie hierher!	Come here!
Kommen Sie mit mir!	Come with me!
Kommen Sie wieder!	Come again!
Kommen Sie nach Hause!	Come home!
Kommen Sie einen Abend!	Come some evening!
Kommen Sie nicht!	Don't come!
Woher kommen Sie?	Where do you come from? Where are you coming from?
Ich komme aus Berlin.	I come from Berlin. I'm coming from Berlin.
Ich komme aus dem Theater.	I'm coming from the theater.
Ich komme sofort.	I'm coming right away.

2. *sagen* to say

ich sage	I say	*wir sagen*	we say
du sagst	you say	*ihr sagt*	you say

er sagt he says	*sie sagen* they say
Man sagt, dass . . .	It's said that . . . People say that . . . They say that . . .
Man hat mir gesagt.	I've been told.
Das ist schwer zu sagen.	That's hard to say.
Sagen Sie!	Say (it)!
Sagen Sie es!	Say it.
Sagen Sie es noch einmal!	Say it again.

Sagen Sie es auf deutsch.	Say it in German.
Sagen Sie es langsam!	Say it slowly!
Sagen Sie es nicht.	Don't say it.
Sagen Sie das nicht.	Don't say that.
Sagen Sie mir . . .	Tell me. Well, tell me. Say, . . .
Sagen Sie, ist das Ihr Ernst?	Say, you're not serious, are you?
Sagen Sie mir.	Tell me.
Sagen Sie es mir.	Say it to me. Tell me it.
Sagen Sie ihm.	Tell him.
Sagen Sie es ihm.	Tell it to him.
Sagen Sie ihm, dass er komme.	Tell him to come.
Sagen Sie es ihm nicht.	Don't tell it to him. Don't tell him.
Sagen Sie ihm nichts.	Don't tell him anything. Tell him nothing.
Sagen Sie es niemand.	Don't tell it to anybody.
Was sagen Sie?	What did you say? ("What say you?")
sozusagen	so to say, so to speak
Können Sie mir sagen, wo ein Hotel ist?	Can you tell me where there's a hotel?
Was möchten Sie sagen?	What do you mean? ("What do you want to say?")
Er hat nichts gesagt.	He hasn't said anything.

QUIZ 28

1. *Ich komme aus dem Theater.*	1. Come with me.
2. *Ich komme sofort.*	2. Where are you coming from?

3.	*Ich komme später.*	3.	Come some evening.
4.	*Woher kommen Sie?*	4.	I'm coming right away.
5.	*Sagen Sie mir.*	5.	I'm coming from the theater.
6.	*Sagen Sie es auf deutsch.*	6.	Say it in German.
7.	*Das ist schwer zu sagen.*	7.	So to say, so to speak.
8.	*Kommen Sie mit mir.*	8.	That's hard to say.
9.	*Kommen Sie einen Abend.*	9.	I'll come later.
10.	*Sozusagen.*	10.	Tell me.

ANSWERS

1—5; 2—4; 3—9; 4—2; 5—10; 6—6; 7—8; 8—1; 9—3; 10—7.

3. *Tun* to do

ich tue	I do	*wir tun*	we do
du tust	you do	*ihr tut*	you do
er tut	he does	*Sie tun*	you do
		sie tun	they do

Ich tue es.	I do it. I'm doing it.
Ich tue es nicht.	I don't do it. I'm not doing it.
Was tun Sie?	What are you doing?
Wie tun Sie das?	How do you do it?
Was haben Sie getan?	What have you done?
Tun Sie es nicht.	Don't do it.
Tun Sie es nicht mehr.	Don't do it any more.
Das ist getan.	It's done. It's over.
Das tut mir weh.	That hurts me.

Ich tue nichts.	I'm not doing anything. I'm doing nothing.
Tun Sie das nicht!	Don't do that.
Tun Sie es noch einmal.	Do it again.
Tun Sie es schnell.	Do it quickly.
Tun Sie nichts!	Don't do anything.
Sie dürfen das nicht tun.	You must not do that.
Ich habe es gerade getan.	I've just done it.
Was tun?	What's to be done? What shall we do? What can be done? ("What to do?")
Wie sollen wir es tun?	How shall we do it?
Wer hat das getan?	Who did that?
Ich weiss nicht was ich tun soll.	I don't know what to do.
So etwas tut man nicht	That isn't done. ("One doesn't do that.")

QUIZ 29

1. *Was haben Sie getan?*	1. Do that!
2. *Tun Sie es nicht.*	2. Do it quickly.
3. *Das ist getan.*	3. What are you doing?
4. *Ich habe es getan.*	4. What have you done?
5. *Was ist zu tun?*	5. Don't do it.
6. *Tun Sie es noch einmal.*	6. That's done. It's over.
7. *Wer hat das getan?*	7. Do me a favor!
8. *Ich habe es gerade getan.*	8. You are hurting me!

9. *Tun Sie mir einen Gefallen!*
9. That isn't done. ("That one does not do.")

10. *Du tust mir weh!*
10. I have done it.

11. *Tun Sie das.*
11. What are we doing tomorrow?

12. *Was tun Sie?*
12. What's to be done? What shall we do?

13. *Tun Sie es schnell.*
13. I've just done it.

14. *So etwas tut man nicht.*
14. Do it again.

15. *Was tun wir morgen?*
15. Who has done that?

ANSWERS

1—4; 2—5; 3—6; 4—10; 5—12; 6—14; 7—15; 8—13; 9—7; 10—8; 11—1; 12—3; 13—2; 14—9; 15—11.

REVIEW QUIZ 8

1. *Ich* _____ (am coming) *sofort.*
   a. *kommen*
   b. *komme*
   c. *sehe*

2. *Das ist schwer zu* _____ (say).
   a. *kommen*
   b. *kommt*
   c. *sagen*

3. *Was* _____ (do) *Sie?*
   a. *sagen*
   b. *tun*
   c. *sagt*

4. *Ich weiss nicht, was ich* _____ (do) *soll.*
   a. *sagen*
   b. *kommen*
   c. *tun*

5. _____ (Take) *Sie es nicht.*
   a. *Nehmen*
   b. *Schicken*
   c. *Versuchen*

6. _____ (Stop) *Sie sofort.*
   a. *Halten*
   b. *Bringen*
   c. *Helfen*

7. *Ich schliesse und* _____ (hope), *bald von Ihnen zu bören.*
   a. *komme*
   b. *hoffe*
   c. *wohne*

8. *Ich* _____ (see) *nicht.*
   a. *sehen*
   b. *wissen*
   c. *sehe*

9. *Ich werde Sie heute abend* _____ (see).
   a. *sehen*
   b. *wisse*
   c. *gesehen*

10. *Er* _____ (holds, is holding) *seinen Hut in der Hand.*
    a. *haltet*
    b. *kann*
    c. *hält*

11. *Ich sehe nicht, wie er das machen* _____ (can).
    a. *könnt*
    b. *kann*
    c. *dann*

12. *Er* _____ (understand) *nicht.*
    a. *konnte*
    b. *versteht*
    c. *stellen*

13. _____ (Take) *Sie Ihr Buch.*
    a. Stellt
    b. Nehmen
    c. Geben

14. *Sie* _____ (owe) *mir nichts.*
    a. schulden
    b. fragen
    c. wartet

15. *Er* _____ (ask) *nichts.*
    a. erwartet
    b. fragt
    c. darf

ANSWERS

1—b; 2—c; 3—b; 4—c; 5—a; 6—a; 7—b; 8—c; 9—a;
10—a; 11—b; 12—b; 13—b; 14—a; 15—b.

82. I'M A STRANGER HERE

Ich Bin Fremd Hier

Ich bin nicht von hier.
I'm not from here.

1. **Verzeihung, mein Herr.**
I beg your pardon, sir.

2. **Bitte sehr.**
Not at all.

3. **Können Sie mir eine Auskunft geben?**
Could you give me some information?

4. **Gewiss, mit Vergnügen.**
Certainly, I'd be glad to.

5. **Ich kenne die Stadt nicht. Ich finde mich nicht zurecht.**
I don't know the town. I can't find my way around.

6. **Das ist doch ganz einfach.**
It's quite simple.

7. **Sehen Sie, ich bin fremd hier.**
You see, I'm a stranger here.

8. **Das macht nichts.**
That's nothing.

9. **Aber, Sie müssen mir doch alles erklären.**
But it is, you have to explain everything to me.

10. **Dann passen Sie auf.**
Then listen to me.

11. **Ich passe auf, mein Herr.**
I'm listening.

12. **Fangen wir mit der Post an.**
Let's begin with the post office.

13. **Schön. Das ist eine gute Idee.**
Fine! That's a good idea.

14. **Sehen Sie das Gebäude an der Ecke?**
Do you see the building at the corner?

15. **Das mit der blauen Laterne?**
The one with the blue lantern?

16. **Ja, das ist es. Das Postamt ist im Erdgeschoss.**
Yes, that's the one. The post office is on the ground floor.

17. **Der Laden mit der Fahne—was ist das?**
The store with the flag—what's that?

18. **Das ist das Polizeiamt.**
That's the police station.

19. **Dort ist ein anderes Gebäude mit einer Fahne.**
There's another building with a flag.

20. **Das ist das Rathaus.**
That's the City Hall.

21. **Wie heisst diese Strasse?**
What's the name of this street?

22. **Marktstrasse. Sehen Sie das Geschäft?**
Market Street. Do you see that store?

23. **Welches? Das auf der rechten Seite?**
Which one? The one on the right?

24. **Ja. Das mit der grossen grünen Kugel im Fenster.**
Yes. The one with a large green globe in the window.

25. **Und einer roten in dem andern?**
And a red one in the other?

26. **Richtig. Das ist die Apotheke.**
That's right. That's the pharmacy.

27. **Ah, ich sehe.**
I see.

28. **Der Doktor wohnt nebenan.**
The doctor lives right next door.

29. **Ist er ein guter Arzt?**
Is he a good doctor?

30. **Ausgezeichnet, er ist jeden Morgen im Krankenhaus.**
Certainly. He's at the hospital every morning.

31. **Wo befindet sich das Krankenhaus?**
Where's the hospital?

32. **Zwei Block von hier, links, gerade bevor Sie auf die Landstrasse kommen.**
Two blocks from here, to your left, just before you come to the main highway.

33. **Gibt es ein Schreibwarengeschäft hier?**
    Is there a stationery store here?

34. **Natürlich. Das ist nicht weit von hier, auf der Hauptstrasse, wo Ihr Hotel ist.**
    Of course. It's not far from here, on Main Street, where your hotel is.

35. **Jetzt bin ich ganz im Bilde.**
    Now I've got my bearings.

36. **Warum kaufen Sie keinen Plan?**
    Why don't you buy a map?

37. **Das ist eine gute Idee! Wo bekomme ich einen?**
    That's a good idea. Where can I get one?

38. **Entweder am Bahnhof oder am Zeitungsstand.**
    Either at the station or at the newspaper stand.

39. **Wo ist der Bahnhof?**
    Where is the station?

40. **Der Bahnhof ist am andern Ende der Marktstrasse.**
    The station is at the other end of Market Street.

41. **Und wo ist ein Zeitungsstand?**
    And where's there a newspaper stand?

42. **An der Ecke.**
    At the corner.

43. **Besten Dank.**
    Thank you very much.

44. **Keine Ursache.**
    Not at all.

45. **Ich hatte Glück, Sie zu treffen. Sie scheinen die Stadt sehr gut zu kennen.**
    I was lucky to meet you. You seem to know the town very well.

46. Das ist selbstverständlich. Ich bin der Bürgermeister der Stadt.
It's quite natural. I'm the mayor of the town.
("It is obvious.")

NOTES

1. *Verzeihung, Entschuldigen Sie, Entschuldigung:* I beg your pardon, Excuse me, I am sorry.
6. *Doch* gives emphasis to the sentence.
8. *Das macht nichts:* "That's nothing." *Das ist unwichtig:* "That's unimportant."
10. *Aufpassen:* "to listen to" or "to watch out" (separable prefix)
12. *Die Post* or *Das Postamt:* the post office.
14. *An der Ecke:* (dative) (no motion toward anything).
20. *Das Rathaus:* "the council house" *Der Bürgermeister:* "the mayor" (Master of the citizens)
25. *Einer roten:* (feminine, dative) because of *mit* in sentence 24.
28. Physicians are called *Doktor* or *Arzt* and are addressed as *Herr Doktor.*
31. *Befindet sich:* "Where does it find itself?" *finden:* to find
32. Note verb transposition.
33. *Das Schreibwarengeschäft:* another example of compound nouns; "store for merchandise to write."
34. Another case of transposition: *wo ihr Hotel ist.*
35. *Jetzt bin ich* . . . (inversion)
38. *Entweder* . . . *oder* either . . . or *weder* . . . *noch* neither . . . nor
43. *Besten Dank* "best thanks"
46. *Selbstverständlich:* "That understands itself"; "That is self evident." (Another polite expression: *Gern geschehen:* "It happened with pleasure.")

QUIZ 30

1. _____ (Not at all).
   a. *Ich bitte Sie*
   b. *Macht nichts*
   c. *Keine Ursache*

2. *Können Sie mir einige Auskünfte* _____
   (give)?
   a. *Vergnügen*
   b. *aber*
   c. *geben*

3. *Sie müssen mir alles* _____ (explain).
   a. *hören*
   b. *erklären*
   c. *anfangen*

4. *Sehen Sie das* _____ (house) *an der Ecke?*
   a. *Haus*
   b. *Gebäude*
   c. *Laterne*

5. *Wie heisst diese* _____ (Street)?
   a. *sehr*
   b. *Strasse*
   c. *Ecke*

6. *Der Arzt* _____ (lives) *nebenan.*
   a. *wohnt*
   b. *singt*
   c. *macht*

7. *Mit einer grossen* _____ (green) *Kugel.*
   a. *roten*
   b. *grünen*
   c. *grün*

8. *Er ist jeden* _____ (morning) *im Hospital.*
   a. *Arzt*
   b. *Morgen*
   c. *Marmor*

9. *Ich hatte* _____ (luck), *Sie zu treffen.*
   a. *danke*
   b. *viel*
   c. *Glück*

10. *Wo befindet sich* _____ (the station)?
   a. *das Postamt*
   b. *der Bahnhof*
   c. *das Rathaus*

ANSWERS

1—c; 2—c; 3—b; 4—a; 5—b; 6—a; 7—b; 8—b; 9—c;
10—b.

LESSON 40

(Conversation)

83. THE COMMONEST VERBS

1. Verbs are divided into two classes:
   Class I weak verbs (regular verbs)
   Class II strong verbs (irregular verbs)

INFINITIVE

PRESENT

I		II	
fragen	to ask	*sprechen*	to speak

PAST

gefragt haben	*gesprochen haben*
to have asked	to have spoken

PARTICIPLES

PRESENT

fragend	asking	*sprechend*	speaking

PAST

gefragt	asked	*gesprochen*	spoken

INDICATIVE

PRESENT

frage	*spreche*
fragst	*sprichst*
fragt	*spricht*
fragen	*sprechen*
fragt	*sprecht*
fragen	*sprechen*

IMPERFECT

fragte	*sprach*
fragtest	*sprachst*
fragte	*sprach*
fragten	*sprachen*
fragtet	*spracht*
fragten	*sprachen*

FUTURE

werde fragen	*werde sprechen*
wirst fragen	*wirst sprechen*
wird fragen	*wird sprechen*
werden fragen	*werden sprechen*
werdet fragen	*werdet sprechen*
werden fragen	*werden sprechen*

CONDITIONAL

würde fragen	würde sprechen
würdest fragen	würdest sprechen
würde fragen	würde sprechen
würden fragen	würden sprechen
würdet fragen	würdet sprechen
würden fragen	würden sprechen

PAST

habe gefragt	habe gesprochen
hast gefragt	hast gesprochen
hat gefragt	hat gesprochen
haben gefragt	haben gesprochen
habt gefragt	habt gesprochen
haben gefragt	haben gesprochen

PLUPERFECT

hatte gefragt	hatte gesprochen
hattest gefragt	hattest gesprochen
hatte gefragt	hatte gesprochen
hatten gefragt	hatten gesprochen
hattet gefragt	hattet gesprochen
hatten gefragt	hatten gesprochen

FUTURE PERFECT

werde gefragt haben	werde gesprochen haben
wirst gefragt haben	wirst gesprochen haben
wird gefragt haben	wird gesprochen haben
werden gefragt haben	werden gesprochen haben
werdet gefragt haben	werdet gesprochen haben
werden gefragt haben	werden gesprochen haben

PAST CONDITIONAL

würde gefragt haben	*würde gesprochen haben*
würdest gefragt haben	*würdest gesprochen haben*
würde gefragt haben	*würde gesprochen haben*
würden gefragt haben	*würden gesprochen haben*
würdet gefragt haben	*würdet gesprochen haben*
würden gefragt haben	*würden gesprochen haben*

IMPERATIVE

frage	*sprich*
fragt	*sprecht*
fragen wir	*sprechen wir*
fragen Sie (sie)	*sprechen Sie (sie)*

SUBJUNCTIVE

PRESENT

dass ich frage	*dass ich spreche*
dass du fragest	*dass du sprechest*
dass er frage	*dass er spreche*
dass wir fragen	*dass wir sprechen*
dass ihr fraget	*dass ihr sprechet*
dass sie fragen	*dass sie sprechen*

IMPERFECT

dass ich fragte	*dass ich spräche*
dass du fragtest	*dass du sprächest*
dass er fragte	*dass er spräche*
dass wir fragten	*dass wir sprächen*
dass ihr fragtet	*dass ihr sprächet*
dass sie fragten	*dass sie sprächen*

PAST

dass ich gefragt habe	*dass ich gesprochen habe*
dass du gefragt habest	*dass du gesprochen habest*
dass er gefragt habe	*dass er gesprochen habe*
dass wir gefragt haben	*dass wir gesprochen haben*
dass ihr gefragt habet	*dass ihr gesprochen habet*
dass sie gefragt haben	*dass sie gesprochen haben*

PLUPERFECT

dass ich gefragt hätte	*dass ich gesprochen hätte*
dass du gefragt hättest	*dass du gesprochen hättest*
dass er gefragt hätte	*dass er gesprochen hätte*
dass wir gefragt hätten	*dass wir gesprochen hätten*
dass ihr gefragt hättet	*dass ihr gesprochen hättet*
dass sie gefragt hätten	*dass sie gesprochen hätten*

2. Some common forms of common verbs:
   a) I have gone, etc.

I have gone

ich bin gegangen	*wir sind gegangen*
du bist gegangen	*ihr seid gegangen*
er ist gegangen	*sie (Sie) sind gegangen*

Compare: *ich habe gegeben* (''I have given'') and *ich bin gegangen* (''I have gone'').

Notice that most verbs use *ich habe, du hast, er hat,* etc., but that a few (chiefly verbs of motion) have *ich bin, du bist, er ist,* etc.

The commonest verbs which have the latter form are:

ich bin eingetreten	I have entered, I entered
ich bin ausgegangen	I have gone out, I went out
ich bin angekommen	I have arrived, I arrived
ich bin abgereist	I have left, I left
ich bin hinaufgegangen	I have gone up, I went up
ich bin hinuntergegangen	I have gone down, I went down
ich bin geblieben	I have remained, I remained
ich bin zurückgekommen	I have returned, I returned
ich bin gefallen	I have fallen, I fell
ich bin geboren	I was born
ich bin geworden	I have become, I became

b) I had given, gone, etc.

I had given

ich hatte gegeben	*wir hatten gegeben*
du hattest gegeben	*ihr hattet gegeben*
er hatte gegeben	*Sie (sie) hatten gegeben*

Other Examples:

ich hatte gesprochen	I had spoken
ich hatte gefragt	I had asked
ich hatte gebracht	I had brought

I had gone

ich war gegangen	*wir waren gegangen*
du warst gegangen	*ihr wart gegangen*
er war gegangen	*Sie (sie) waren gegangen*

Other Examples:

ich war angekommen	I had arrived
ich war gekommen	I had gone
ich war eingetreten	I had entered
ich war ausgegangen	I had gone out
ich war abgereist	I had left
ich war hinaufgegangen	I had gone up
ich war gefallen	I had fallen

c) Help! Bring

Helfen Sie mir!	Help me!
Bringen Sie mir noch mehr . . .	Bring me some more . . .
Bringen Sie es mir!	Bring it to me.
Halten Sie!	Stop!
Halten Sie sofort!	Stop right away!
Halten Sie dort!	Stop there!
Halten Sie ihn!	Stop him!
Setzen Sie sich!	Sit down! Have a seat!
Glauben Sie mir!	Believe me!
Hören Sie!	Listen!
Hören Sie mir zu.	Listen to me.
Hören Sie mir gut zu.	Listen to me carefully.
Hören Sie sich das an.	Listen to this (that).
Hören Sie gut zu.	Listen carefully.

The *Sie* form corresponds to the polite, that is, the formal form.
The familiar form, that is, the *du* form, is as follows:

	geben "to give"
du gibst	you give
Gib!	Give!

	sprechen "to speak"
du sprichst	you speak
Sprich!	Speak!

nehmen "to take"

du nimmst	you take
Nimm!	Take!

d) Giving, Speaking

gebend	giving
sprechend	speaking
kommend	coming
sehend	seeing
Fliessendes Wasser	Running water
Den Sitten folgend	Following the custom

Notice that the *-end* form corresponds to our "-ing" form in English.

e) Let's

Gehen wir dorthin.	Let's go over there.
Sehen wir einmal.	Let's see.
Gehen wir!	Let's leave!
Versuchen wir!	Let's try!
Warten wir!	Let's wait!
Nehmen wir etwas!	Let's take some!
Hören Sie ihm zu.	Listen to him.
Hören Sie ihm nicht zu.	Don't listen (to him).
Nehmen Sie das fort.	Take that away.
Herein!	Come in!
Treten Sie ein!	Go in! Come in! Enter!
Schicken Sie es ihm.	Send it to him.
Schicken Sie sie mir.	Send them to me.
Schicken Sie ihm einige!	Send him some!
Schicken Sie mir einige!	Send me some!
Versuchen Sie!	Try!
Versuchen Sie nicht!	Don't try!
Versuchen Sie nicht, das zu tun!	Don't try to do that!

Waschen Sie sich!	Wash yourself!
Stehen Sie auf!	Get up! Stand up!
Lesen Sie das!	Read that!
Führen Sie mich dorthin!	Take me there!
Gehen Sie dort hinauf!	Go up there!
Zeigen Sie mir!	Show me!
Zeigen Sie mir das!	Show me it (that)!
Zeigen Sie ihm!	Show him!
Zeigen Sie es ihm nicht!	Don't show it to him!
Vergessen Sie nicht!	Don't forget!
Gehen Sie fort!	Leave!
Gehen Sie schnell fort!	Leave quickly! Go right away!
Gehen Sie hinein!	Go in!
Denken Sie daran!	Think of it!
Tragen Sie das dorthin!	Carry this over there!
Nehmen Sie!	Take!
Nehmen Sie es!	Take it!
Nehmen Sie es nicht!	Don't take it!
Nehmen Sie noch eins!	Take another one!
Nehmen Sie den Zug!	Take the train!
Nehmen Sie ein Taxi.	Take a taxi.
Sehen Sie!	Look!
Sehen Sie noch einmal!	Look again!
Sehen Sie hierher!	Look here!
Sehen Sie mich an!	Look at me!
Sehen das an!	Look at this (that)!
Sehen Sie nicht hierher!	Don't look!
Geben Sie es mir wieder!	Return it to me!
Gehen Sie nach Hause!	Go home!
Gehen Sie früh nach Hause!	Go home early!
Wiederholen Sie!	Repeat! Say it again!
Wiederholen Sie das!	Repeat it (this, that). Say it (this, that) again.

Bleiben Sie!	Stay!
Bleiben Sie hier!	Stay here!
Bleiben Sie ruhig!	Be still! (quiet, calm)
Gehen Sie hinaus!	Go out!
Folgen Sie!	Follow!
Folgen Sie mir!	Follow me!
Folgen Sie ihm!	Follow him!
Berühren Sie es nicht!	Don't touch it!
Schenken Sie mir Kaffee ein.	Pour me some coffee.

QUIZ 32

1. *Zeigen Sie mir.*		1. Look at (that).
2. *Treten Sie ein!*		2. Look here.
3. *Darf ich?*		3. Take a taxi.
4. *Denken Sie daran.*		4. Take another one.
5. *Nimm! Nehmen Sie!*		5. Take it.
6. *Nimm es!*		6. Take!
7. *Nehmen Sie ein Taxi.*		7. May I?
8. *Nehmen Sie noch eins.*		8. Think of it.
9. *Sehen Sie her.*		9. Go in!
10. *Sehen Sie das an.*		10. Show me.

ANSWERS

1—10; 2—9; 3—7; 4—8; 5—6; 6—5; 7—3; 8—4; 9—2; 10—1.

84. MEETING AN OLD FRIEND

Zwei alte Freunde treffen sich.
Two old friends meet.

1. **M.: Oh! Sie sind es! Wie geht es Ihnen, alter Freund!**
   M.: Oh, there you are! How are you?

2. **W.: Und Ihnen, mein Lieber?**
   W.: How are you? (my dear)

3. **M.: Sind Sie nicht zu sehr ermüdet von Ihrer Reise?**
   M.: Not too tired from your trip?

4. **W.: Keineswegs.**
   W.: Not at all.

5. **M.: Darf ich Sie mit meiner Frau bekannt machen?**
   M.: I'd like you to meet my wife.

6. **W.: Mit Vergnügen.**
   W.: I'd be very happy to.

7. **M.: Liebes, das ist Herr Wagner.**
   M.: This is Heinrich Wagner, dear.

8. **W.: Sehr erfreut, Sie kennenzulernen.**
   W.: I'm very happy to know you.

9. **Frau M.: Ganz meinerseits.**
   Mrs. M.: The pleasure is mine.

10. **W.: Ich freue mich wirklich, Sie wirderzusehen.**
    W.: It's really good to see you again.

11. **M.: Ich auch. Sie haben sich überhaupt nicht verändert.**
    I'm certainly glad, too. You haven't changed a bit.

12. **W.: Sie aber auch nicht.**
    Neither have you.

13. **Frau M.: Gefällt es Ihrer Frau Gemahlin in den Vereinigten Staaten?**
    Mrs. M.: Does Mrs. Wagner like the United States?

14. **W.: Sehr gut.**
    W.: She likes it a lot.

15. **Frau M.: Es ist sicher ganz anders als in Berlin?**
Mrs. M.: It must be quite different from Berlin?

16. **W.: Es gibt bestimmt eine Menge merkwürdiger Dinge in den Vereinigten Staaten.**
W.: There certainly are lots of very curious things in the United States!

17. **Frau M.: Zum Beispiel?**
Mrs. M.: For example?

18. **W.: Zum Beispiel, Sie würden bestimmt nicht auf den Gedanken kommen, in einer Apotheke Mittag zu essen.**
W.: For example, it certainly wouldn't occur to you to have lunch in a pharmacy.

19. **M.: Das ist wohl ein Scherz.**
M.: You're joking!

20. **W.: Gar nicht, ich meine es sehr ernst.**
W.: Not at all, I'm very serious.

21. **Frau M.: Wie bitte? Erzählen Sie uns das. Sie sagen . . . man isst zu Mittag in einer Apotheke.**
Mrs. M.: Come, tell us about it! You say . . . one has lunch . . . in a pharmacy.

22. **W.: Ja, gnädige Frau, sogar ein Beefsteak. . . .**
W.: Yes, you can even have a steak. . . .

23. **M.: In einer Apotheke?**
M.: In a pharmacy?

24. **W.: Ja, in einer Apotheke, und als Nachtisch können Sie ausgezeichnetes Eis haben.**
W.: Yes, in a pharmacy—and you can have excellent ice cream for dessert.

25. **Frau M.: Aber der Geruch der Apotheke—
    stört Sie das nicht?**
    Mrs. M.: But the smell of the pharmacy—
    doesn't it bother you?

26. **W.: Es gibt keinen Geruch in unsern...**
    W.: There isn't any smell in our...

27. **M.: Apotheken?**
    M.:... pharmacies?

28. **W.: Übrigens nennen wir Sie nicht Apotheken sondern "drug stores."**
    W.: No, ("Moreover") we don't call them
    pharmacies but "drug stores."

29. **M.: Ah! Deshalb! Sie geben ihnen einen andern Namen!**
    M.: Oh! That's the trick! They give them a
    different name!

30. **Frau M.: Aber was ändert das?**
    Mrs. M.: But how does that change things?

31. **M.: Dann ist es eben keine Apotheke mehr!**
    M.: Then it's no longer a pharmacy!

32. **W.: Sie finden eine Menge anderer Dinge in einem "drug store." Spielsachen, Briefmarken Zigaretten, Bonbons...**
    W.: You also find many other things in a drug
    store: toys, stamps, cigarettes, candy...

33. **M.: Das ist wirklich komisch!**
    M.: That's really very funny.

34. **W.: Bücher, Schreibpapier, Küchengeräte, Toilettenartikel und wer weiss was noch...**
    W.: Books, stationery, cooking utensils, toilet
    articles and what-have-you.

35. **M.: Dann ist es also ein Kaufhaus!**
    M.: It's a bazaar, then!

36. **W.: Nein, es ist eben ein "drug store"!**
    W.: No, it's just a drug store!

NOTES

1. *Sie sind es:* idiomatic expression for "There you are." Notice the use of the capital in the pronouns *Sie* and *Ihnen* because Herr Müller is addressing Herr Wagner.
2. *Mein Lieber:* "Old fellow," used generally only to someone you know well.
5. *Bekannt machen:* "to make acquainted" also *Gestatten Sie, dass ich Sie bekannt mache.* "Allow me to introduce you."
8. *Kennenlernen:* to get acquainted ("to learn to know").
9. *ganz meinerseits:* "Quite reciprocal."
10. *sich freuen:* to rejoice. *wiedersehen*—to see again (separable prefix)
13. *Gefällt es Ihrer Frau Gemahlin . . . !* Does it please your wife . . . ?
18. Conditional of *kommen. (würden . . . kommen)*
19. *Sie machen einen Scherz:* "You are making a joke."
28. *sondern:* is used instead of *aber* after a negation.
31. Inversion after *dann.*
34. *Wer weiss was noch:* "Who knows what more" infinitive: *wissen (see table page . . .)*

QUIZ 33

1. *Wie lange waren Sie* _____ (there)?
   a. *dessen*
   b. *hier*
   c. *dort*

2. _____ (How) *geht's, mein lieber Freund?*
   a. *Dort*
   b. *Wie*
   c. *Ihr*

3. *Nicht zu* _____ (tiring), *diese Reise?*
   a. *Welt*
   b. *erfindend*
   c. *ermüdend*

4. *Ich werde Sie meiner* _____ (wife) *vorstellen.*
   a. *Frau*
   b. *Freude*
   c. *frei*

5. *Es* _____ (pleases) *mich sehr, sie wiederzusehen.*
   a. *wechselt*
   b. *freut*
   c. *selbst*

6. *Es gibt wirklich komische* _____ (things).
   a. *sehr*
   b. *dieser*
   c. *Dinge*

7. *Ich meine es* _____ (very) *ernst.*
   a. *sehr*
   b. *aber*
   c. *ganz*

8. *Wir* _____ (call) *sie nicht Apotheken.*
   a. *nennen*
   b. *nehmen*
   c. *waren*

9. *Sehr erfreut, Sie* _____ ("to learn to know").
   a. *gehen zu können*
   b. *kennenzulernen*
   c. *Bekanntschaft*

ANSWERS

1—c; 2—b; 3—c; 4—a; 5—b; 6—c; 7—a; 8—a; 9—a;

85. THE COMMONEST VERBS (Continued)

1. *sehen* to see; to look

ich sehe	*wir sehen*
du siehst	*ihr seht*
er sieht	*Sie (sie) sehen*

Sehen wir einmal nach.
Let's see. ('Let's see once after it'')

Ich sehe nicht.
I don't see.

Er sieht alles.
He sees everything

Haben Sie ihn gesehen?
Have you seen him?

Ich habe sie gerade gesehen.
I've just seen her.

Wen sehen Sie?
Whom do you see?

Können Sie mich jetzt sehen?
Can you see me now?

2. *wissen* to know

ich weiss	*wir wissen*
du weisst	*ihr wisst*
er weiss	*Sie (sie) wissen*

Ich weiss es.
I know it.

Ich weiss es nicht.
I don't know it.

Ich weiss es sehr gut.
I know it very well.

Er weiss nichts.
He doesn't know anything.

Ich weiss nichts darüber.
I don't know anything about it.

Ich weiss, dass er hier ist.
I know that he is here.

Wissen Sie das?
Do you know that?

Wissen Sie, wo er ist?
Do you know where he is?

Wer weiss?
Who knows?

Er weiss nicht mehr darüber als Sie.
He doesn't know any more about it than you do.

Wir wissen nicht, ob er kommt.
We don't know, whether he is coming.

3. *halten* to hold

ich halte	*wir halten*
du hältst	*ihr haltet*
er hält	*Sie (sie) halten*

Halten Sie mir das einen Moment.
Hold this for me a minute.

Er hält seinen Hut in der Hand.
He's holding his hat in his hand.

Halten Sie fest!
Hold on firmly!

Bleiben Sie am Apparat!
Hold the wire a minute.

Halten Sie still!
Keep still! Don't move!

Er hält es für selbstverständlich.
He takes it for granted.

Was halten Sie davon?
What do you think about it?

Ich halte nicht viel davon.
I don't think much of it.

Halten Sie rechts.
Keep to your right.

Halten Sie Ihr Versprechen!
Keep your promise!

4. *können* to be able; can

ich kann	*wir können*
du kannst	*ihr könnt*
er kann	*Sie (sie) können*

Ich kann nicht.
I can't.

Ich kann es tun.
I can do it.

Können Sie mir sagen, ob...
Can you tell me whether...

Können Sie kommen?
Can you come?

Ich verstehe nicht, wie er das kann.
I don't see how he can do that.

Ich kann nicht auf die Frage antworten.
I can't answer the question.

Sie können es ohne Schwierigkeit tun.
You can do it without any difficulty.

Ich kann nicht dorthin gehen.
I can't go there.

Wann können wir gehen?
When can we leave?

Sie können dorthin gehen.
You can go there.

Können Sie mir helfen?
Can you help me?

5. *verstehen* to understand

ich verstehe	*wir verstehen*
du verstehst	*ihr versteht*
er versteht	*Sie (sie) verstehen*

Er versteht nicht.
He doesn't understand.

Ich verstehe sehr gut.
I understand very well.

Ich verstehe Sie nicht.
I don't understand you.

Verstehen Sie mich nicht?
Don't you understand me?

Verstehen Sie?
Do you understand?

Verstehen Sie Deutsch?
Do you understand German?

Verstehen Sie Englisch?
Do you understand English?

Verstehen Sie alles, was er Ihnen sagt?
Do you understand everything he's saying to you?

Ich habe nicht verstanden.
I don't understand, ("I haven't understood. I
  didn't understand.")

Haben Sie verstanden?
Did you understand? ("Have you understood?")

Er versteht nichts vom Geschäft.
He doesn't understand anything about business.

Verstanden?
Did you understand? Do you understand? ("Is that
  understood?")

Ich verstehe überhaupt nichts.
I don't understand it at all. I don't understand
  anything about it.

6. *legen*	to put in a prone position
stellen	to put in a standing position
hinstellen	to put down

Stellen Sie es dorthin.
Put it there.

Wo haben Sie es hingestellt?
Where did you put it?

Legen Sie es hin.
Lay it down.

Er weiss nie, wo er seine Sachen hinlegt.
He never knows where he puts his things.

Stellen Sie den Schirm in die Ecke.
Put the umbrella in the corner.

Legen Sie das Buch auf den Tisch.
Put the book on the table.

7. *kennen* to know

ich kenne	*wir kennen*
du kennst	*ihr kennt*
er kennt	*Sie (sie) kennen*

Ich kenne ihn.
I know him.

Ich kenne es nicht.
I don't know it.

Kennen Sie dieses Wort?
Do you know this word?

Ich kenne seine Familie.
I know his family.

Jeder kennt es.
Everybody knows it.

Ich kenne ihn dem Aussehen nach.
I know him by sight.

Ich kenne ihn dem Namen nach.
I know him by name.

Das ist sehr bekannt.
It's very well known.

Das ist nicht sehr bekannt in Deutschland.
That's not very well known in Germany.

Das ist unbekannt.
It's unknown.

8. *wollen* to want

ich will	*wir wollen*
du willst	*ihr wollt*
er will	*Sie (sie) wollen*

Ich will es.
I want it. I insist on it.

Ich will es nicht.
I don't want it.

Ich will nichts.
I don't want anything.

Ich will etwas.
I want some ("something").

Er will nichts davon.
He doesn't want any of it.

Er kann es tun, aber er will nicht.
He can do it but he doesn't want to.

Wollen Sie?
Do you want to?

Was wollen Sie?
What do you want? (not very polite)

Was möchten Sie?
What do you want (wish)? What would you like?

Wollen Sie kommen?
Do you want to come?

Wollen Sie mit uns kommen?
Do you want to come with us?

Wollen Sie Samstag kommen?
Do you want to come Saturday?

Wollen Sie mit uns zu Mittag essen?
Will you have lunch with us?

Wer will das?
Who wants that?

Was wollen Sie sagen?
What do you want to say?

Wollen Sie mir folgen?
Will you follow me?

Wie Sie wollen.
As you wish.

Wenn Sie wollen.
If you wish. If you want to.

9. *müssen* to have to; to be obliged to; must

ich muss	*wir müssen*
du musst	*ihr müsst*
er muss	*Sie (sie) müssen*

Ich muss jetzt gehen.
I must (have to) go now.

Er muss kommen.
He must (has to) come.

Er muss hier sein.
He must (has to) be here.

Sie müssen dort sein.
They have to (should, ought to) be there.

Müssen Sie dort hingehen?
Do you have to go (there)?

Was muss ich tun?
What do I have to do?

10. *warten* to wait

Warten Sie hier.
Wait here.

Warten Sie dort.
Wait there.

Warten Sie auf mich.
Wait for me.

Warten Sie ein wenig.
Wait a little.

Warten Sie einen Moment.
Wait a minute.

Warten Sie nicht.
Don't wait.

Ich warte auf ihn.
I'm waiting for him.

Sie wartet auf die andern.
She's waiting for the others.

Auf wen warten Sie?
Whom are you waiting for?

Warum warten Sie?
Why are you waiting?

Es tut mir leid, dass ich sie habe warten lassen.
I'm sorry I kept you waiting.

11. *fragen* to ask

Fragen Sie dort drüben.
Ask over there.

Was fragt er?
What's he asking? What does he want?

Fragen Sie nach dem Weg, wenn Sie sich verlaufen.
Ask your way if you get lost.

Fragen Sie ihn, wie spätes ist.
Ask him the time (what time it is).

Gehen Sie und fragen Sie ihn.
Go and ask him.

Wenn jemand nach mir fragt, ich komme gleich zurück.
If someone asks for me, I'll be back in a moment.

Er hat gefragt, wo es ist.
He asked where it is.

Was man weiss, soll man nicht fragen.
What one knows, one should not ask.

Fragen Sie nicht so viel!
Don't ask so much!

Jemand fragt nach Ihnen.
Someone is asking for you. You're wanted.

Ich frage mich, ob das wahr ist.
I wonder if it's true. ("I ask myself if . . .")

Ich frage mich, warum er nicht kommt.
I wonder why he doesn't come.

Das frage ich mich selbst.
I wonder about that. ("That's what I am asking
   myself.")

12. *lieben* to love

gern haben	to like
lieber haben	to prefer

Er liebt sie.
He loves her. He's in love with her.

Haben Sie ihn gern?
Do you like him?

Das habe ich nicht gern.
I don't like that.

Ich habe das andere lieber.
I like the other better. I prefer the other.

Ich gehe lieber heute abend dorthin.
I'd rather go there this evening.

13. *wert sein* to be worth

Wieviel ist das wert?
How much is that worth?

Das ist keinen Pfennig wert.
That's not worth a cent.

Das ist nichts wert.
That's not worth anything. That's no good.

Das ist nicht viel wert.
That's not worth much.

Das ist preiswert.
That's reasonable. ("It's worth its price.")

Das ist viel Geld wert.
That's worth a lot of money.

Das ist es nicht wert.
It's not worth that.

86. COMMON NOTICES AND SIGNS

Bekanntmachung	Public Notice
Herren	Gentlemen
Damen	Ladies
Herren Toilette	Men's Room
Damen Toilette	Ladies' Room
W.C.	Toilet
Nichtraucher	Non-Smokers
Rauchen verboten!	No Smoking
Offen	Open
Geschlossen	Closed
Eingang	Entrance
Ausgang	Exit
Notausgang	Emergency Exit
Fahrstuhl	Elevator
Erdgeschoss	Ground Floor
Drücken	Push
Ziehen	Pull
Drehen	Turn
Bitte schellen (Klingeln)	Please Ring

Durchgang verboten!	Keep Out! No Thoroughfare!
Herein!	Come In!
Herein ohne zu klopfen.	Come In Without Knocking.
Klopfen	Knock
Vor Eintritt klopfen.	Knock Before Entering.
Wegen Umbauten geschlossen.	Closed For Repairs.
Unter neuen Leitung.	Under New Management.
Eintritt verboten!	No Admittance!
Eröffnung in Kürze	Will Open Shortly
Ganze Nacht geöffnet	Open All Night
Es ist verboten, auf den Boden zu spucken.	No Spitting!
Füsse abputzen	Wipe your feet
Hunde an der Leine	Keep your Dogs On Leash
Für Fussgänger verboten	Pedestrains Keep Out!
Betreten des Geländes verboten	No Trespassing
Beschwerdebüro	Complaint Department
Am Schalter fragen	Apply at the Window
Wechselstube	Money Exchanged
Zu verkaufen	For Sale
Zu vermieten	For Rent
Wohnung zu vermieten	Unfurnished Apartment to Let
Möblierte Wohnung zu vermieten	Furnished Apartment to Let
Preisnachlass	Reductions
Ausverkauf	Sale
Garderobe	Check Room (in a hotel, restaurant or cafe)
Billiard Zimmer	Billiard Room

Hausmeister	Janitor
Abstellraum	Cloakroom
Umleitung	Detour
Strassenarbeiten	Road under Repair
Gefährliche Kurve	Dangerous Curve
Parken verboten	No Parking
Einbahnstrasse	One-Way Street
Überschreiten der Gleise verboten!	Do not Cross the Tracks!
Eisenbahnkreuzung	Railroad Crossing
Eisenbahnstrecke	Railroad
Unterführung	Underpass
Halt!	Stop!
Vorsicht!	Caution!
Fussgänger	Pedestrian Crossing
Kreuzung	Crossroads
Omnibushaltestelle	Bus Stop
Plakate ankleben verboten!	Post No Bills!
Höchstgeschwindigkeit 30 Stundenkilometer	Maximum Speed 30 Kilometers Per Hour
Langsam fahren!	Go Slow!
Schule	School—Go Slow
Gefahr!	Danger!
Frisch gestrichen	Fresh Paint
Haltestelle	Stops Here (Stop)
Nicht aus dem Fenster lehnen!	Don't Lean Out of the Window!
Alarm Signal	Alarm Signal
Hochspannung	High Voltage
Untergrundbahn	Subway
Gepäckaufbewahrung	Baggage Room, Check Room (in a railroad station)
Wartesaal	Waiting Room
Erste Klasse	First Class
Zweiter Klasse	Second Class
Dritter Klasse	Third Class

Ankunft	Arrival
Abfahrt	Departure
Bahnsteig	Platform
Auskunft	Information
Theaterkasse	Box Office
Postamt	Post Office
Briefkasten	Mail Box
Kartenschalter	Ticket Office
Feuerlöscher	Fire Box
Bücherei, Bibliothek	Public Library
Polizeiramt	Police Station
Tankstelle	Gas Station
Buchhandlung	Bookstore
Rathaus	City Hall
Herren und Damen Frisör	Barber Shop and Hair Dresser
Arzt	Physician
Zahnarzt	Dentist
Schumacher	Shoe Repairing
Matinee	Matinee
Abendvorstellung um 8:30	Evening Performance at 8:30
Abendkleidung	Formal Dress
Strassenkleidung	Informal Dress
Laufende Vorstellung	Continuous Performance
Programmwechsel	Change of Program
Erfrischungen	Refreshments

FINAL QUIZ

1. _____ (How) *geht es Ihnen?*
   a. *Wann*
   b. *Wie*
   c. *Wenn*

2. _____ (Speak) *Sie langsam.*
   a. *Sprechen*
   b. *Sprecht*
   c. *Sprich*

3. _____ (Have) *Sie Zigaretten?*
   a. *Habe*
   b. *Hast*
   c. *Haben*

4. *Geben Sie* _____ (me) *die Speisekarte.*
   a. *mir*
   b. *mich*
   c. *es*

5. _____ (I'd like) *eine Tasse Kaffee.*
   a. *Ich will*
   b. *Ich möchte*
   c. *Ich gehe*

6. *Wir möchten für drei Personnen* _____
   (breakfast).
   a. *Mittagessen*
   b. *Frühstück*
   c. *Abendessen*

7. _____ (Bring) *Sie mir einen Teelöffel.*
   a. *Geben*
   b. *Bringen*
   c. *Können*

8. *Wo befindet sich* _____ (the station)?
   a. *der Weg*
   b. *der Bahnhof*
   c. *das Büro*

9. _____ (Are you) *sicher?*
   a. *Machen Sie*
   b. *Sagen Sie*
   c. *Sind Sie*

10. _____ (I have) *genug Zeit.*
    a. *Ich bin*
    b. *Ich habe*
    c. *Ich hatte*

11. _____ (Does he have) *Geld?*
     a. *Es gibt*
     b. *Ist er*
     c. *Hat er*

12. _____ (Are there) *Briefe für mich?*
     a. *Es gibt*
     b. *Gibt es*
     c. *Hat er*

13. _____ (Understand) *Sie?*
     a. *Verstehe*
     b. *Verstehen*
     c. *Hören*

14. *Ich bin* _____ (glad) *Sie kennenzulernen.*
     a. *glücklich*
     b. *erfreut*
     c. *geehrt*

15. *Wollen Sie davon wenig oder* _____ (a lot)?
     a. *noch*
     b. *viel*
     c. *genug*

16. *Was* _____ (say) *Sie?*
     a. *machen*
     b. *sagen*
     c. *gesagt*

17. *Wie* _____ (does one say) *das auf deutsch?*
     a. *sagen Sie*
     b. *sagt man*
     c. *schreibt man*

18. *Ihre Telefonnummer ist MITTE* _____
     (3-30-74).
     a. *drei dreiundzwanzig vierundfünfzig*
     b. *drei dreissig vierundsiebzig*
     c. *drei einunddressig achtundsiebzig*

19. _____ (I need) *das.*
   a. *Ich möchte*
   b. *Ich habe davon*
   c. *Ich brauche*

20. *Ich komme* _____ (tomorrow morning).
   a. *nachmittag*
   b. *morgen früh*
   c. *gestern abend*

21. _____ (Must one) *den Hausmeister deshalb sehen?*
   a. *Müssen*
   b. *Muss man*
   c. *Musst du*

22. *Ich* _____ (beg) *Sie um Verzeihung.*
   a. *bitte*
   b. *frage*
   c. *sage*

23. *Wie* _____ (is your name) *Sie?*
   a. *heissen*
   b. *fragen*
   c. *wissen*

24. _____ (The check), *bitte.*
   a. *Die Butter*
   b. *Das Geld*
   c. *Die Rechnung*

25. *Würden Sie mir eine Serviette* _____ (give)?
   a. *bringen*
   b. *geben*
   c. *gehen*

ANSWERS

1—b; 2—a; 3—c; 4—a; 5—b; 6—b; 7—b; 8—b; 9—c;
10—b; 11—c; 12—b; 13—b; 14—b; 15—b; 16—b;
17—b; 18—b; 19—c; 20—b; 21—b; 22—a; 23—a;
24—c; 25—b.

WHEN YOU GET 100% ON THIS QUIZ YOU CAN CONSIDER THAT YOU HAVE MASTERED THE COURSE.

SUMMARY OF GERMAN GRAMMAR

1. THE ALPHABET

Letter	Name	Letter	Name	Letter	Name
a	ah	j	yot	s	ess
b	beh	k	kah	t	teh
c	tseh	l	ell	u	oo
d	deh	m	em	v	fauh
e	eh	n	en	w	veh
f	eff	o	oh	x	iks
g	gay	p	peh	y	üpsilonn
h	hah	q	ku	z	tsett
i	ee	r	err		

2. THE VOWELS

a	as in *ah* "father"
ä	as in "fair"
e	as in *ay* "may"
ee or eh	like the *a* in "care"
e	as in *er* "manner"
i	as in "ship"
o	as in "lone"
o	as in "love"
ö	similar to the *e* in *geben*
u	as in *u* "good"
ü	as in *ee* "see" (plus rounded lips)
y	as in "typical"

3. THE DIPTHONGS

ai	
ei	*y* "by"
au	as in *ou* "house"
äu	
eu	as in *oy* "boy"

4. THE CONSONANTS

b	as in *b* "bed" and at the end of a word as in *p* "trap"
c	as in *k* "keep" and rather rarely like *ts*
d	as in *d* "date" at the end of a word like *t* as in "but"
f	as in *f* "fly"
g	as in *g* "garden"
h	as in *h* "hundred" sometimes not pronounced at all as in *Schuh*—"shoe"
j	as in *y* "York"
k	as in *c* "cut"
l	as in *l* "life"
m	as in *m* "man"
n	as in *n* "never"
p	as in *p* "painter"
q	as in *q* "quality"
r	is a little more rolled than in English.
s	at the beginning of a word as in *z* "zoo" at the end of a word or syllable as in *s* "son"
t	as in *t* "tea"
v	as in *f* "fair"
w	as in *v* "vain"
x	as in *x* "mix"
z	like the English combination *ts*.

5. SPECIAL LETTER COMBINATIONS

ch   as in *k* "character"

chs   as in *ks Fuchs*—"fox"

ch   a sound near the English *h* in "hue": *Kirche*—church

ch   a guttural sound not exisiting in English but close to the Scotch "loch"; *e.g. ach!*—"ah!"

ig   as sound of *h* in "hue"

sch   as in *sh* "shoe"

sp or st when placed at the beginning of the word also gives the initial sound of the *sh* as in "shoe" *e.g. Spanien*—"Spain"

ng   as in *ng* "sing"

tz   is similar to the English *ts, e.g. Blitz*—"lightning"

6. THE GERMAN DECLENSION

1. Nominative (subject, noun)

Das Buch ist hier.   The book is here.

2. Genitive (possessive case)
der Name des Lehrers   The name of the teacher

3. Dative (indirect object)
Er gibt dem Kind einen   He gives an apple to the
*   Apfel.*   child.

4. Accusative (direct object)
Sie hält die Feder.   She is holding the pen.

7. PLURAL OF NOUNS

1. Masculine

   a) nominative plus *e*

der Abend	*die Abende*
der Freund	*die Freunde*

   b) nominative plus *er*

der Geist	*die Geister*
der Leib	*die Leiber*

   c) nominative plus *e* and ¨ (Umlaut) on the last vowel

der Hut	*die Hüte*
der Fall	*die Fälle*

   d) nominative plus *er* and ¨ (Umlaut) on the last vowel

der Mann	*die Männer*
der Rand	*die Ränder*

   e) masculine nouns ending in *el, en, er* do not change.

der Schlüssel	*die Schlüssel*
der Kuchen	*die Kuchen*
der Maler	*die Maler*

A certain number of masculine nouns, most of them ending in *e*, form all their cases by the addition of an *n* or *en*.

der Knabe	*die Knaben*
der Mensch	*die Menschen*

2. Feminine

   a) Most feminine nouns form their plural by adding *n* or *en*

die Tür	*die Türen*
die Frage	*die Fragen*

   b) Some add *e* or ¨ (Umlaut) on the last vowel
      and an *e*.

die Kenntnis	*die Kenntnisse*
die Frucht	*die Früchte*

   c) Feminine words ending in *in* form their
      plural in *innen*

die Schülerin	*die Schülerinnen*
die Freundin	*die Freundinnen*

3. Neuter

   Most neuter nouns form their plural like the
   masculine, the majority of them in *e* or *er*.

das Heft	*die Hefte*
das Licht	*die Lichter*

8. GENDER

German nouns can be either masculine, feminine, or
neuter. However, there is no definite rule to deter-
mine their gender. Here are a few helpful hints:

1. Masculine are:

   a) designations of trade or profession
      der Maler, der Arzt

   b) titles of nobility
      der Fürst, der Graf

   c) nouns ending in *ling*:
      der Sperling, der Jüngling

2. Feminine are:

   a) feminine designations of trade:
      die Malerin, die Ärztin

   b) feminine titles of nobility:
      die Königin, die Fürstin

   c) names of numbers:
      eine Drei, eine Null

d) many names of trees:
   die Tanne, die Eiche

e) nouns ending in *ei, heit, keit, schaft, sucht, ung*
   die Freiheit, die Gesellschaft, die Ahnung

3. Neuter are:

   a) the diminutives in *chen* or *lein:*
      das Mädchen   das Büblein

   b) many nouns ending in *tum:*
      das Altertum

   c) most nouns of metals:
      das Gold, das Eisen

   d) most cities:
      das schöne Berlin

   e) most countries:
      das Amerika

   f) colors:
      das Rot

   g) most collective nouns beginning with *ge:*
      das Gebirge (mountains)

THE STRESS: German words generally have one strongly accented syllable or even two if the word is very long.

1. *Short words:* The accent is generally on the first syllable:
   Example: *Váter, Mútter, Brúder*

2. *Long words:* the accent is generally on the root of the word:
   Emp**feh**lung Ge**bir**ge Ge**bäu**de

3. Separable prefixes are always accented:
   abmachen **zu**geben **mit**gehen

4. Inseparable prefixes (*be, emp, ent, er, ge, ver, zer*) are never accented. The accent always falls on the following syllable.
erhálten vergéssen zerbréchen

9. THE DEFINITE ARTICLE

1. Unlike English usage, the definite article can be used in front of a first name (*familiar*)
Der Hans und die Margarete John and Margaret

2. In front of a title:
Ist der Herr Doktor da? Is the (Mr.) doctor at home? *Nein, aber die Frau Doktor ist zu Hause.* No, but the (Mrs.) Doctor is at home.

Remember the declension of the articles

MASCULINE	FEMININE	NEUTER
N. *der*	N. *die*	N. *das*
G. *des*	G. *der*	G. *des*
D. *dem*	D. *der*	D. *dem*
A. *den*	A. *die*	A. *das*

PLURAL FOR ALL:
N. *die*
G. *der*
D. *den*
A. *die*

10. THE INDEFINITE ARTICLE

Notice that in a negation *ein* becomes *kein*.

Er war kein Arzt, sondern ein Zahnarzt.
He was not a physician but a dentist.

MASCULINE	FEMININE	NEUTER
N. *ein*	*eine*	*ein*
G. *eines*	*einer*	*eines*
D. *einem*	*einer*	*einem*
A. *einen*	*eine*	*ein*

Masculine, feminine and neutral singular of *kein,* same as *ein.*

PLURAL
keine
keiner
keinen
keine

11. THE ADJECTIVES

Adjectives are declined in three ways:

1. Without article or pronoun (strong declension):

MASCULINE	FEMININE	NEUTER
roter Wein	*rote Tinte*	*rotes Gold*
roten Weines	*roter Tinte*	*roten Golds*
rotem Wein	*roter Tinte*	*rotem Gold*
roten Wein	*rote Tinte*	*rotes Gold*

PLURAL (M.F.N.)
Nom. *rote Weine*
Gen. *roter Weine*
Dat. *roten Weinen*
Acc. *rote Weine*

2. With the definite article (Weak Declension):

SINGULAR

N. *der rote Wein*	N. *die rote Tinte*
G. *des roten Weines*	G. *der roten Tinte*
D. *dem roten Wein*	D. *der roten Tinte*
A. *den roten Wein*	A. *die rote Tinte*

PLURAL

das rote Gold   N. *die roten Weine*
des roten Goldes   G. *der roten Weine*
dem roten Gold   D. *den roten Weinen*
das rote Gold   S. *die roten Weine*

3. With the indefinite article (Mixed Declension):

MASCULINE   FEMININE

N. *ein roter Wein*   seine rote *Tinte*
G. *eines roten Weines*   seiner roten Tinte
D. *einem roten Wein*   seiner roten Tinte
A. *einen roten Wein*   seine rote *Tinte*

NEUTER
N. *kein rotes Gold*
G. *keines roten Goldes*
D. *keinem roten Gold*
A. *kein rotes Gold*

PLURAL
N. *meine roten Weine*
G. *meiner roten Weine*
D. *meinen roten Weinen*
A. *meine roten Weine*

12. COMPARATIVE AND SUPERLATIVE

1. The comparative and the superlative are formed as in English by adding *er* for the comparative and *st* (or *est*) for the superlative to the adjective.

   Some short adjectives also take ¨ (Umlaut) on their vowels.

schlecht, schlechter,	bad, worse, worst
schlechtest	
alt, älter, ältest	old, older, oldest

2. There are a few adjectives which have an irregular comparative. Here are the most common ones:

gut	*besser*	*der (die, das) beste*
gross	*grösser*	*der (die, das) grösste*
hoch	*höher*	*der (die, das) höchste*
nahe	*näher*	*der (die, das) nächste*

13. THE PARTITIVE

1. Generally not translated:

Example:
Geben Sie mir Brot. Give me some bread.
Geben Sie mir ein Glas Wein. Give me a glass of wine.

2. *Etwas* can also be used to mean a part of something:

Example:
Ich gebe ihm etwas zu trinken.
I am giving him something to drink.

Ich gebe ihm etwas davon.
I give him some of it.

3. The negative *kein:* is declined like the indefinite article.

Example:
Ich habe ein Messer, aber keine Gabel.
I have a knife but no fork.

14. POSSESSIVE ADJECTIVES

1. Possessive adjectives agree in gender and number with the thing possessed:

   NOMINATIVE

   Before Singular nouns:

MASCULINE AND NEUTER		FEMININE
mein	my	*meine*
dein	your (*fam.*)	*deine*
sein	his, its	*seine*
ihr	her	*ihre*
unser	our	*unsere*
euer	your (*fam. plural*)	*eure*
Ihr	your (*polite*)	*Ihre*
ihr	their	*ihre*

   PLURAL

   meine
   deine
   seine
   ihre
   unsere
   eure
   Ihre
   ihre

2. Examples:

mein Hund	my dog
meine Tante	my aunt
ihr Vater	her father
seine Mutter	his mother
Ihr Buch	your (*polite*) book
ihre Bleistifte	their pencils

3. Notice that these adjectives agree in gender not with the possessor as in English, but with the noun they modify. *Sein* and *seine* may therefore mean "his" or "its":

Hans spricht mit seiner Mutter.
John is talking to his mother.

Das Bier hat seinen Geschmack verloren.
The beer has lost its taste.

15. POSSESSIVE PRONOUNS

NOMINATIVE

MASCULINE	FEMININE	NEUTER	
meiner	*meine*	*meines*	mine
deiner	*deine*	*deines*	yours (*fam.*)
seiner	*seine*	*seines*	his
ihrer	*ihre*	*ihres*	hers
unser	*unsere*	*unseres*	ours
euer	*eure*	*eures*	yours (*fam.*)
Ihrer	*Ihre*	*Ihres*	yours (*polite*)
ihrer	*ihre*	*ihres*	theirs

Ist das mein Hut?—Ja, das ist Ihrer.
Is that my hat?—Yes, that is yours.

Ist das deine Krawatte?—Ja, das ist meine.
Is that your tie?—Yes, that is mine.

Ist das sein Buch?—Nein, das ist meins.
Is that his book?—No, that is mine.

Ist das ihr Schirm?—Nein, das ist seiner.
Is that her umbrella?—No, that is his.

16. DEMONSTRATIVE ADJECTIVE

SINGULAR

N. *dieser*	*diese*	*dieses*	
G. *dieses*	*dieser*	*dieses*	
D. *diesem*	*dieser*	*diesem*	this or *that
A. *diesen*	*diese*	*dieses*	

PLURAL (M, F, N)   Examples:

N. *diese*   *Dieses Haus ist schön.*

G. *dieser*   This (that) house is

D. *diesen*   beautiful.

A. *diese*

Jenes Haus ist bässlich.
That house is ugly.

*jen(er,-e,-es) may also be used, but is less
common in conversation.

17. DEMONSTRATIVE PRONOUNS

derjenigen	*diejenige*	*dasjenige*
desjenigen	*derjenigen*	*desjenigen*
demjenigen	*derjenigen*	*demjenigen*
denjenigen	*diejenige*	*dasjenige*
	diejenigen	
	derjenigen	
	denjenigen	
	diejenigen	

*Mein Buch ist blau. Dasjenige meiner Schwester ist
grün.*

18. RELATIVE PRONOUNS

The relative pronoun is like the demonstrative pronoun but its declension varies in the Genitive singular
of all genders, and in the Genitive and Dative plural.

N.	*der*	*die*	*das*	who
G.	*dessen*	*deren*	*dessen*	whose
D.	*dem*	*der*	*dem*	to whom
A.	*den*	*die*	*das*	whom

PLURAL:

N.	*die*	who
G.	*deren*	whose
D.	*deren*	to whom
A.	*die*	whom

Ex:

Der Junge, dessen Vater ich kenne,...
The boy whose father I know...

Welcher can also be used and is declined in same way as the article *der.*

Ex:

Der Freund, welcher morgen kommt,...
The friend who is coming tomorrow...

NOTES

1. These pronouns must agree in gender and number with the noun they refer to.

   Das Mädchen, das in der Strasse spielt.
   The little girl who is playing on the street.

2. A comma should always be used before them.
3. The verb is always placed at the end of the sentence it introduces.
4. They can never be omitted as in English.

   Das Buch, das ich lese.
   The book (that) I am reading.

19. PERSONAL PRONOUN

SINGULAR

N.	*ich*	*du*	*er*	*sie*	*es*
G.	*meiner*	*deiner*	*seiner*	*ihrer*	*seines*
D.	*mir*	*dir*	*ihm*	*ihr*	*ihm*
A.	*mich*	*dich*	*ihm*	*sie*	*es*

PLURAL

N.	*wir*	*ihr*	*Sie*	*sie*
G.	*unserer*	*eurer*	*Ihrer*	*ihrer*
D.	*uns*	*euch*	*Ihnen*	*ihnen*
A.	*uns*	*euch*	*Sie*	*sie*

Examples:

Wir geben ihr Blumen.
We are giving her flowers.

Du sprichst mit ihm.
You are speaking with him.

Wir sprechen von Ihnen.
We're talking about you (*polite*).

Wessen werde ich gedenken? Deiner.
Whom will I think of? You.

20. THE INDEFINITE PRONOUN

man	one
jedermann	everybody, everyone
jemand	somebody, someone
niemand	nobody
etwas	something, some

Examples:

Jemand steht vor der Tür.
Someone is standing before the door.

Es muss etwas geschehen.
Something has to be done.

21. POSITION OF PRONOUNS

In the sentence the indirect object generally precedes the direct object.

Example:

Er gibt dem Kind ein Buch.
He is giving the child a book.

However, when these two objects are pronouns the direct object comes first.

Example:

Er gibt es ihm.
He is giving it to him.

22. THE NEGATIVE

A sentence is made negative by using the word *nicht*, generally following the verb. Words may come between the verb and *nicht*.

Ich weiss.	I know.
Ich weiss nicht.	I do not know.
Ich weiss es nicht.	I don't know it.

The negative of *ein* is *kein*.

23. ADVERBS

1. Almost all adjectives can be used as adverbs.
2. Their comparative is formed the same way as the adjectives.
   Their superlative is preceded by *am* instead of the article.

Fritz ist ein guter Tänzer.
Fritz is a good dancer.
Fritz tanzi gut.
Fritz dances well.

Karl ist ein besserer Tänzer als Fritz.
Karl is a better dancer than Fritz. Karl dances
   better than Fritz.

Fred Astaire ist der beste Tänzer.
Fred Astaire is the best dancer.

Fred Astaire tanzt am besten.
Fred Astaire dances better than all of them.

3. A few adverbs have an irregular comparative
   and superlative. Here are the most common
   ones:

viel	mehr	am meisten	much, more, most
gern	lieber	am liebsten	gladly, preferably, most preferably
bald	eher	am ehsten	soon, sooner, soonest

4. Adverbs of place:

hier	here
dort	there
daneben, neben	beside, next to
weg	aside, away
davor, vor	before
hinter	behind
darauf	on top
darunter, unter	underneath
darin, drinnen	inside
draussen	outside
überall	everywhere
nirgendwo, nirgends	nowhere
weit	far
nahe	near
wo	where
woanders	elsewhere
dort oben	up there
dort drüben	over there

5. Adverbs of time:

heute	today

morgen	tomorrow
gestern	yesterday
vorgestern	the day before yesterday
übermorgen	the day after tomorrow
jetzt	now
dann	then
vorher	before
damals	once, at that time
einmal, ehemals	once, formerly
früh	early
bald	soon
spät	late
oft	often
niemals, nie	never
immer, je, jemals	always, ever
lang, lange	long, for a long time
sofort	at once, right away
manchmal	sometimes
noch	still, yet
nicht mehr	no longer, no more

6. Adverbs of manner:

gut	well
schlecht	ill, badly
so, somit	thus, so
ähnlich	similarly
andererseits	on the other hand
zusammen	together
viel	much, very
besonders	above all, especially
absichtlich	on purpose, purposely
ausdrücklich	expressly
gewöhnlich	usually

7. Adverbs of quanitity or degree:

viel	much, many
genug	enough

kaum	not much, hardly
wenig	little
mehr	more
nicht mehr	no more
weniger	less
noch mehr	more, even more
zuviel	too much, too many
soviel	so much, so many

24. PREPOSITIONS

1. With the Genitive:

während	during
wegen	because of
statt, anstatt	instead of
trotz	in spite of

2. With the Accusative:

durch	through, by
für	for
gegen	against, toward
ohne	without
um	round, about, at (time)

3. With the Dative:

aus	from, out of
bei	at, by, near, with
mit	with
nach	after, to (a place)
seit	since
von	of, from, by
zu	to, at

4. With the Dative or Accusative:

an	at, to
auf	on, upon, in
hinter	behind
in	in, into, at

neben	beside, near
über	over, across
unter	under, among
vor	before, ago
zwischen	between

25. CONTRACTIONS

am	for	*an dem*
im	for	*in dem*
beim	for	*bei dem*
vom	for	*von dem*
zum	for	*zu dem*
zur	for	*zu der*
ins	for	*in das*

26. PREFIXES

Many German verbs have certain prefixes. They are divided into three groups:

1. *The inseparable prefixes,* which remain attached to the verb and are never accented (just like the English verbs: overthrow, understand, etc.). In the past tense, the past participles of these verbs do not take the prefix *ge*. These prefixes are: *be, emp, ent, er, ge, miss, ver, zer, hinter, wider.*

2. *The separable prefixes:* These are linked to the verb in the compound tenses; in the other tenses they are separated and generally placed at the end of the sentence. They are always accented. The most common such prefixes are: *ab, an, auf, aus, bei, ein, fort, mit, nach, vor, weg, zu, frei, los, wahr, statt.* There are also compound separable prefixes added to verbs, such as: *hinaús, heraúf, hinéin, heréin zurück, zusammen.*

   her indicates a movement toward the person who is speaking:

Kommen Sie herunter. Come down.

hin indicates a movement away from the person speaking:

Geh hinaús! Go out!

The separable prefix is so important in the sentence that the verb is sometimes omitted in short statements:

Die Tür zu! Close the door! ("The door closed")

Heréin! (Come) in!

3. Some prefixes are sometimes separable and sometimes inseparable, depending on the meaning of the verb. They are:

wieder, voll, durch, um, unter, über.

Examples: *Der Schüler wiederholt seine Lektion.*
        The student repeats his lesson.

Holen Sie das wieder! Take it back!

*Er schenkte unsere
    Gläser voll.* He filled our glasses.

Er vollendet sein Werk. He accomplishes his work.

27. THE TENSES OF THE INDICATIVE

Simple Tenses

1. The present tense expresses an uncompleted action in the present. It has several English translations:

ich spreche I speak, I am speaking, I do speak

ich esse I eat, I am eating, I do eat

2. The imperfect tense expresses a continued or habitual action in the past. It also indicates an action that was happening when something else happened. The weak verbs add the following endings to their stem: *te, test, te, tet, ten.*

The strong verbs usually change their stem vowel. The first and third person singular have no ending. The others are as in the present.

Er schlief, als Hans eintrat.	He was sleeping when John entered.
Er sprach oft davon.	He often spoke about that.
Es war dunkel, als er ausging.	It was night (dark) when he went out.

3. The future tense is formed by using the auxiliary *werden* plus the infinitive of the verb. It indicates a future action:

Er wird morgen ankommen.	He'll arrive tomorrow.
Ich werde ihm morgen schreiben.	I'll write him tomorrow.

4. The past tense is formed by adding the past participle to the present indicative of *haben* or, in some cases, *sein*. It is used to indicate a past action which is completed in the present or which happened only once:

Er hat mir nichts gesagt.	He didn't tell me anything.
Ich habe meine Arbeit beendet.	I finished my work. I have finished my work.
Haben Sie ihn gesehen?	Have you seen him?
Sie sind angekommen.	They arrived.

5. The pluperfect tense is formed by adding the past participle to the imperfect of *haben* or, in some cases, *sein*. It translates the English pluperfect:

Er hatte es getan.	He had done it.
Als ich zurückkam, war er gegangen.	When I came back, he had gone.

6. The future perfect tense is formed by adding the past participle to the future of *haben* or, in some cases, *sein*. It translates the English future perfect:

| *Er wird bald seine Arbeit beendet haben.* | He will soon have finished his work. |

Sometimes it indicates probability:

Er wird es ihm zweifellos gesagt haben.	No doubt he will have told him.
Er wird krank gewesen sein.	He probably was sick.
Ich werde mich geirrt haben.	I must have been mistaken.

Compound tenses

1. The compound tenses are made up of *haben* (intransitive verbs use *sein*) and the part participle:

| *Er hat gesprochen.* | He has spoken. |
| *Sie haben gegessen.* | You have eaten. |

2. Most compound tenses are formed with the auxiliary *haben*:

| *Ich habe ein Geschenk erhalten.* | I received a present. |
| *Er hat zuviel getrunken.* | He drank too much. |

3. The most common intransitive verbs conjugated with the verb *sein* are:
   gehen, ankommen, absteigen, eintreten, einsteigen, sterben, abreisen, bleiben, kommen, fallen, zurückkommen, laufen

Examples:

Ich bin gekommen.	I have come.
Er ist angekommen.	He has come.
Wir sind abgereist.	We have left.

28. THE PAST PARTICIPLE

The first syllable of the past participle of the weak and strong verbs is always *ge* when the verbs have no prefix whatsoever. If they do have a separable prefix, then the syllable *ge* stands between the prefix and the

past participle. If the verbs have an inseparable prefix, the past participle has no additional *ge*.

Infinitive	*Past Participle*

(strong verb without prefix)

   ziehen to pull   *gezogen*

(strong with a separable prefix)

   vorziehen to prefer   *vorgezogen*

(weak without prefix)

   warten to wait   *gewártet*

(weak with a separable prefix)

   abwarten to wait   *abgewartet*
      and see

(strong verb with an inseparable prefix)

   verlieren to lose   *verlóren*

(weak with an inseparable prefix)

   entdecken to discover   *entdéckt*

In the weak verbs, the part participle ends in *t* or *et*.

   arbeiten   *gearbeitet*
   lernen   *gelernt*

In the strong verbs the past participle ends in *en*, but
the vowel of the infinitive stem generally changes.
Therefore when you study the verbs, do not forget to
memorize the past participle as well as the other
tenses. See table of irregular verbs, (No. 40).

29. USE OF THE AUXILIARIES HABEN and SEIN

Notice that most verbs form the perfect, pluperfect
and future perfect with the auxiliary *haben:*

   ich habe gesehen   I have seen

(chiefly transitive & reflexive)

   du hast gesehen   you have seen
   ich habe mich   I have washed myself.
     gewaschen

However, quite a few verbs, chiefly intransitive, form
these tenses with the auxiliary *sein:*

  1. The verbs *sein, werden, bleiben*.

2. Verbs indicating a change of place (chiefly, verbs of motion, as: *gehen, kommen, eilen, fallen, fliessen, laufen, reisen, rollen, steigen, sinken, aufstehen, flogen, begegnen,* etc.

3. Verbs indicating a change in the condition of a thing or a person, as: *aufwachen, einschlafen, wachsen, aufbleiben, verblühen, vergehen, verschwinden, sterben, erhalten, platzen, erkranken.*

30. THE SUBJUNCTIVE

Present of *haben, sein, werden* "to have, to be, shall"

ich habe	*ich sei*	*ich werde*
du habest	*du seiest*	*du werdest*
er habe	*er sei*	*er werde*
wir haben	*wir seien*	*wir werden*
ihr habet	*ihr seiet*	*ihr werdet*
sie haben	*sie seien*	*sie werden*

The endings of both weak and strong verbs are *e, est, e, en, et, en.* The strong verbs keep the stem vowel in each person.

Imperfect

ich hätte	*ich wäre*	*ich würde*
du hättest	*du wärest*	*du würdest*
er hätte	*er wäre*	*er würde*
wir hätten	*wir wären*	*wir würden*
ihr hättet	*ihr wäret*	*ihr würdet*
sie hätten	*sie wären*	*sie würden*

Notice that the imperfect tense of the weak verbs has the same endings both in the indicative and subjunctive.

Example:

er lernte he learned   subj: *dass er lernte* that he learned

Strong verbs have the same endings as the present subjunctive, but take the *Umlaut* if their stem vowel is *a*, *e*, or *u*.

ich tat I did   *ich täte* that I did

The past tenses: The past, pluperfect, and the future are formed with the past participle of the indicative of the verb plus the auxiliaries *haben*, *sein*, and *werden* in their respective subjunctive forms. The subjunctive is used to express "doubt, wish, eventuality, unreality." It is also used:

1. in indirect discourse
2. after certain conjunctions and expressions, such as:

damit so that   *als ob* as if
es sei denn, dass   unless

Examples:

Er glaubte, dass er käme	He believed that he was coming.
Wir helfen ihm, damit er gesund werde.	We help him, so that he may be healthy again.

3. After the conjunction *wenn* to indicate a conditional; in this case it is often replaced by the conditional mood.

Wenn ich ein Vogel wäre, flöge ich.
If I were a bird, I would fly.

4. To express a wish:

Mögen Sie glücklich sein!	May you be happy!
Wärest du doch hier!	Wish you were here!

31. THE CONDITIONAL

The conditional is formed with the auxiliary *werden* in its imperfect subjunctive form.

ich würde	*wir würden*
du würdest	*ihr würdet*
er würde	*sie (Sie) würden*

It is generally used in connection with the conjunction *wenn* instead of the subjunctive to express a condition. *Wenn wir Geld hätten, würdenuir eine weite Reise machen.*

If we had any money, we would go on a long trip.

The past conditional is formed like the past future, but using *würde* instead of *werde*.

32. THE PASSIVE VOICE

The passive voice is formed with the past participle of the verb and the auxiliary *werden* used in the present and in the past.

    Die Erde wird von der Sonne beleuchtet.

    The earth is lit by the sun. "By" is translated by
       the German *von* (plus dative):

    Amerika wurde von Kolumbus entdeckt.

    America was discovered by Columbus.

In the past tense (perfect tense) the participle of the auxiliary *werden*, *geworden*, drops the prefix *ge* and becomes simply *worden*

Example:

    Das Buch ist von ihm geschrieben worden.

    The book has been written by him.

33. THE IMPERATIVE

The imperative of the verbs is formed from the present indicative tense.

2nd person singular: Drop the ending *n* from the infinitive. However, strong verbs changing the vowel *e* to *i* or *ie* in the present indicative form their imperative by dropping the *st* from this tense.

Lerne! (du lernst)

Nimm! (du nimmst)

1st person plural: Invert the infinitive form with the personal pronoun:

Singen wir! (wir singen)

2nd person plural: Simply insert the second person plural of the present indicative tense and omit the pronoun.

Gebt! (ihr gebt)

3rd person plural: Same as the 1st person plural

Nehmen Sie geben Sie

To express the imperative, the verb *lassen* can also be used; it corresponds to the English "let."

Example:
Lassen Sie das sein!	Let it be!

Imperative of *sein* and *haben:*

sein to be	*haben* to have
sei (fam.) be	*habe* (fam.) have
seid (fam. pl.) be	*habt* (fam. pl.) have
seien wir let us be	*haben wir* let us have

34. THE INFINITIVE

The infinitive is usually preceded by *zu* when used in connection with another verb; however, *zu* is omitted when the infinitive is used in connection with the following verbs:

werden, können, dürfen, wollen, mögen, müssen, sollen, lassen, machen, hören, sehen, heissen, helfen, lehren, lernen

Examples:
Er bittet ihm, den Brief zu schreiben.	He asks him to write the letter.
Ich werde schreiben.	I shall write. (Future)
Ich helfe ihm aufladen.	I'm helping him load.
Er lehrt uns schwimmen.	He teaches us to swim.

The infinitive is also used after certain conjunctions in connection with *zu:*

um . . . zu (so that)	(in order to) sometimes
ohne . . . zu (without)	the *zu* can be used
anstatt . . . zu (instead of)	alone

Examples:

Wir leben, um zu arbeiten.	We live in order to work.
Ich kann nicht essen, ohne zu trinken.	I cannot eat without drinking.
Er faulenzt, anstatt uns zu helfen.	He is lazy instead of helping us.

Words with a separable prefix have the *zu* between the prefix and the infinitive.

Example: *aufmachen*
Er bittet ihn, die Tür aufzumachen.
He asks him to open the door.

35. COMPLEMENTS OF VERBS

Verbs can be followed by:
a) preposition: their complement should be put in the case required by the preposition; for example:
bedecken mit—"to cover with" (always dative)

| *Der Tisch ist mit Staub bedeckt.* | The table is covered with dust. |

b) an object without a preposition: The genitive, accusative, or dative is used, depending on the verb.

Examples: (Genitive)

| *Er ist des Mordes beschuldigt.* | He is accused of murder. |

(Dative)

| *Sie glauben mir nicht.* | You don't believe me. |

(Accusative)

| *Wir lieben ihn.* | We love him. |

36. CHANGES IN THE NORMAL SEQUENCE OF WORDS WITHIN A SENTENCE

1. *By Transposition:* putting the verb at the end of a sentence.

In a subordinate clause, that is, a sentence beginning with a relative pronoun or a conjunction, the verb is always placed at the end of the sentence.

Die Sprache, die wir lernen, ist Deutsch.

The language that we are learning is German.

Ich kann nicht sehen, weil es dunkel ist.

I cannot see because it is dark.

Ich glaube, dass das Essen in diesem Restaurant gut ist.

I believe that the food in this restaurant is good.

Notice also that a comma is always used before the relative pronoun and the conjunction. If the verb is in a compound tense the *auxiliary* is placed at the end of the sentence.

Ich glaube nicht, dass es morgen regnen wird.

I do not believe that it will rain tomorrow.

In the case of an indirect interrogation or subordinate clause introduced by an interrogative word, such as the pronouns: *wer, was,* or *welcher,* or the adverbs: *wo, wann, etc.,* or the conjunction: *ob,* the verb is also placed at the end of the sentence.

Wir wissen nicht, ob er morgen kommt.

We don't know whether he is coming tomorrow.

Können Sie mir sagen, wie weit es von hier bis zum Bahnhof ist?

Can you tell me how far it is from here to the station?

2. *By Inversion:* putting the verb before the subject. The inversion is necessary:

a) usually when a question is asked. (affirmative)

Er schreibt den Brief.   He writes the letter.

(interrogative)

Schreibt er den Brief?   Does he write the
                                    letter?

b) in the main clause of any sentence when it is
preceded by a subordinate clause.

*Wir können nicht sehen, wenn wir die Augen
schliessen.*

We cannot see, when we close our eyes.

No inversion occurs because the subordinate clause is
put after the main clause.

*Wenn wir die Augen schliessen, können wir nicht
sehen.*

If we close our eyes, we cannot see.

In the above example, however, you have the inversion because the subordinate clause is put before the
main clause.

c) whenever the main clause opens with a word
other than the subject.

*Die Kinder werden morgen ins (in das) Kino
gehen.*

The children will go to the movies tomorrow.

The above does not take any inversion because the
sentence is started by its subject, *die Kinder.*

Morgen werden die Kinder ins Kino gehen.

Tomorrow the children will go to the movies.

Here we have inversion because the sentence does not
start with its subject, *die Kinder,* but with another
word: *morgen.*

37. INDIRECT DISCOURSE

When you want to tell a story or make an indirect
quotation in German, you use indirect discourse:

Hans sagt: "Ich gehe zum Bahnhof."

John says, "I am going to the station."

Indirect:

Hans sagt, dass er zum Bahnnhof gehe.

John says that he is going to the station.

Imperfect:

Hans sagte, dass er zum Bahnhof ginge.

John said that he was going to the station.

Notice:

1. The subjunctive should be used (even though you can use the indicative, as many Germans do).
2. The conjunction *dass*—"that" can be used or omitted.

If it is used, the verb should be placed at the end of the sentence, as in the regular case of transposition.

Er sagt, dass er zum Bahnhof gehe.

3. If it is omitted, the order of the words remains unchanged.

Hans sagt, er gehe zum Bahnhof.

John says he is going to the station.

Hans sagte, er ginge zum Bahnhof.

John said he was going to the station.

4. Notice that in both instances, a comma is used at the beginning of the second clause.
5. The following sequence of tenses is generally observed:

Principal verb in the
  present indicative   second clause
  future indicative   present subjunctive

Principal clause in the past, present conditional, past subjunctive

Principal clause in the pluperfect, past conditional, pluperfect subjunctive

38. CONSTRUCTION OF THE SENTENCE
(Summary)

1. Main Clauses or Simple Sentences:
   a) Affirmative sentence:

Das Buch ist rot.   The book is red.

b) Interrogative:

Ist das Buch rot?   Is the book red?

c) Negative:

Das Buch ist nicht rot.   The book is not red.

d) Past tenses:

Ich habe ein Gedicht gelernt.   I have learnt a poem.

e) Infinitive:

Sie brauchen das nicht zu wissen.   You do not need to know that.

2. Subordinate clauses:

a) Transposition:

Ich sehe, dass das Buch rot ist.   I see that the book is red.

Ich kenne den Schuler, der das Gedicht liest.   I know the student who is reading the poem.

b) Inversion:

Wenn das Wetter schön ist, gehe ich gern spazieren.

When the weather is fine, I like to take a walk.

c) Indirect discourse:

Sie antwortet ihm, dass sie eine Schülerin $\begin{cases} sei. \\ ist \end{cases}$

Sie antwortet ihm, sie $\begin{cases} sei \\ ist \end{cases}$ *eine Schülerin.*

She answers (him) that she is a pupil.

39. THE MOST COMMON IRREGULAR VERBS

sein   to be

INFINITIVE

PRESENT	PAST
sein	*gewesen sein*

PARTICIPLES

PRESENT	PAST
seiend	*gewesen*

INDICATIVE

PRESENT	PAST
bin	*bin gewesen*
bist	*bist gewesen*
ist	*ist gewesen*
sind	*sind gewesen*
seid	*seid gewesen*
sind	*sind gewesen*

IMPERFECT	PLUPERFECT
war	*war gewesen*
warst	*warst gewesen*
war	*war gewesen*
waren	*waren gewesen*
wart	*wart gewesen*
waren	*waren gewesen*

FUTURE	PAST FUTURE
werde sein	*werde gewesen sein*
wirst sein	*wirst gewesen sein*
wird sein	*wird gewesen sein*
werden sein	*werden gewesen sein*
werdet sein	*werdet gewesen sein*
werden sein	*werden gewesen sein*

CONDITIONAL

PRESENT	PAST
würde sein	*würde gewesen sein*
würdest sein	*würdest gewesen sein*
würde sein	*würde gewesen sein*
würden sein	*würden gewesen sein*
würdet sein	*würdet gewesen sein*
würden sein	*würden gewesen sein*

IMPERATIVE

sei
seien wir
seid
seien Sie

SUBJUNCTIVE

PRESENT   PAST

dass ich sei   *dass ich gewesen sei*
dass du seist   *dass du gewesen seist*
dass er sei   *dass er gewesen sei*

dass wir seien   *dass wir gewesen seien*
dass ihr seiet   *dass ihr gewesen seid*
dass wir seien   *dass sie gewesen seien*

IMPERFECT

dass ich wäre   *dass ich gewesen wäre*
dass du wärest   *dass du gewesen wärest*
dass er wäre   *dass er gewesen wäre*

dass wir wären   *dass wir gewesen*
                              wären
dass ihr wäret   *dass ihr gewesen wäret*
dass sie wären   *dass sie gewesen wären*

haben   to have

INFINITIVE

PRESENT   PAST

haben   *gehabt haben*

PARTICIPLES

PRESENT	PAST
habend	*gehabt*

INDICATIVE

PRESENT	PAST
habe	*habe gehabt*
hast	*hast gehabt*
hat	*hat gehabt*
haben	*haben gehabt*
habt	*habt gehabt*
haben	*haben gehabt*

IMPERFECT	PLUPERFECT
hatte	*hatte gehabt*
hattest	*hattest gehabt*
hatte	*hatte gehabt*
hatten	*hatten gehabt*
hattet	*hattet gehabt*
hatten	*hatten gehabt*

FUTURE	FUTURE PERFECT
werde haben	*werde gehabt haben*
wirst haben	*wirst gehabt haben*
wird haben	*wird gehabt haben*
werden haben	*werden gehabt haben*
werdet haben	*werdet gehabt haben*
werden haben	*werden gehabt haben*

CONDITIONAL	PAST CONDITIONAL
würde haben	*würde gehabt haben*
würdest haben	*würdest gehabt haben*
würde haben	*würde gehabt haben*
würden haben	*würden gehabt haben*
würdet haben	*würdet gehabt haben*
würden haben	*würden gehabt haben*

IMPERATIVE

habe
haben wir
habt
haben Sie

SUBJUNCTIVE

PRESENT	PAST
dass ich habe	*dass ich gehabt habe*
dass du habest	*dass du gehabt habest*
dass er habe	*dass er gehabt habe*
dass wir haben	*dass wir gehabt haben*
dass ihr habet	*dass ihr gehabt habet*
dass sie haben	*dass sie gehabt haben*

IMPERFECT	PLUPERFECT
dass ich hätte	*dass ich gehabt hätte*
dass du hättest	*dass du gehabt hättest*
dass er hätte	*dass er gehabt hätte*

dass wir hätten	*dass wir gehabt hätten*
dass ihr hättet	*dass ihr gehabt hättet*
das sie hätten	*dass sie gehabt hätten*

werden to become

INFINITIVE

PRESENT	PAST
werden	—

PARTICIPLES

PRESENT	PAST
werdend	*geworden*

INDICATIVE

PRESENT	PAST
werde	*bin geworden*
wirst	*bist geworden*
wird	*ist geworden*
werden	*sind geworden*
werdet	*seid geworden*
werden	*sind geworden*

IMPERFECT	PLUPERFECT
wurde	*war geworden*
wurdest	*warst geworden*
wurde	*war geworden*

wurden	waren geworden
wurdet	wart geworden
wurden	waren geworden

FUTURE

werde werden	**FUTURE PERFECT**

werde werden	werde geworden sein
wirst werden	wirst geworden sein
wird werden	wird geworden sein
werden werden	werden geworden sein
werdet werden	werdet geworden sein
werden werden	werden geworden sein

CONDITIONAL

PAST CONDITIONAL

würde werden	würde geworden sein
würdest werden	würdest geworden sein
würde werden	würde geworden sein
würden werden	würden geworden sein
würdet werden	würdet geworden sein
würden werden	würden geworden sein

IMPERATIVE

werde
werden wir
werdet
werden Sie

SUBJUNCTIVE

PRESENT

IMPERFECT

dass ich werde	dass ich würde
dass du werdest	dass du würdest
dass er werde	dass er würde

dass wir werden	*dass wir würden*
dass ihr werdet	*dass ihr würdet*
dass sie werden	*dass sie würden*

können   to be able to

INFINITIVE

PRESENT	PAST
können	*gekonnt haben*

PARTICIPLES

PRESENT	PAST
konnend	*gekonnt*

INDICATIVE

PRESENT	PAST
kann	*habe gekonnt*
kannst	*hast gekonnt*
kann	*hat gekonnt*
können	*haben gekonnt*
könnt	*habt gekonnt*
können	*haben gekonnt*

IMPERFECT	PLUPERFECT
konnte	*hatte gekonnt*
konntest	*hattest gekonnt*
konnte	*hatte gekonnt*

konnten	hatten gekonnt
konntet	hattet gekonnt
konnten	hatten gekonnt

FUTURE	**FUTURE PERFECT**
werde können	werde gekonnt haben
wirst können	wirst gekonnt haben
wird können	wird gekonnt haben
werden können	werden gekonnt haben
werdet können	werdet gekonnt haben
werden können	werden gekonnt haben

CONDITIONAL	**PAST CONDITIONAL**
würde können	würde gekonnt haben
würdest können	würdest gekonnt haben
würde können	würde gekonnt haben
würden können	würden gekonnt haben
würdet können	würdet gekonnt haben
würden können	würden gekonnt haben

SUBJUNCTIVE

PRESENT	**PAST**
dass ich könne	dass ich gekonnt habe
dass du könnest	dass du gekonnt habest
dass er könne	dass er gekonnt habe
dass wir können	dass wir gekonnt haben
dass ihr könnet	dass ihr gekonnt habet
dass sie können	dass sie gekonnt haben

IMPERFECT	PLUPERFECT
dass ich könnte	dass ich gekonnt hätte
dass du könntest	dass du gekonnt hättest
dass er könnte	dass er gekonnt hätte
dass wir könnten	dass wir gekonnt hätten
dass ihr könntet	dass ihr gekonnt hättet
dass sie könnten	dass sie gekonnt hätten

<u>dürfen</u>   to be allowed to

INFINITIVE

PRESENT	PAST
dürfen	gedurft haben

PARTICIPLES

PRESENT	PAST
	gedurft

INDICATIVE

PRESENT	PAST
darf	habe gedurft
darfst	hast gedurft
darf	hat gedurft
dürfen	haben gedurft
dürft	habt gedurft
dürfen	haben gedurft

IMPERFECT	PLUPERFECT
durfte	*hatte gedurft*
durftest	*hattet gedurft*
durfte	*hatte gedurft*
durften	*hatten gedurft*
durftet	*hattet gedurft*
durften	*hatten gedurft*

FUTURE	FUTURE PERFECT
werde dürfen	*werde gedurft haben*
wirst dürfen	*wirst gedurft haben*
wird dürfen	*wird gedurft haben*
werden dürfen	*werden gedurft haben*
werdet dürfen	*werdet gedurft haben*
werden dürfen	*werden gedurft haben*

CONDITIONAL	PAST CONDITIONAL
würde dürfen	*würde gedurft haben*
würdest dürfen	*würdest gedurft haben*
würde dürfen	*würde gedurft haben*
würden dürfen	*würden gedurft haben*
würdet dürfen	*würdet gedurft haben*
würden dürfen	*würden gedurft haben*

SUBJUNCTIVE

PRESENT	PAST
dass ich dürfe	*dass ich gedurft habe*
dass du dürfest	*dass du gedurft habest*
dass er dürfe	*dass er gedurft habe*

dass wir dürfen	dass wir gedurft haben
dass ihr dürfet	dass ihr gedurft habet
dass sie dürfen	dass sie gedurft haben

IMPERFECT	PLUPERFECT
dass ich dürfte	dass ich gedurft hätte
dass du dürftest	dass du gedurft hättest
dass er dürfe	dass er gedurft hätte
dass wir dürften	dass wir gedurft hätten
dass ihr dürftet	dass ihr gedurft hättet
dass sie dürften	dass sie gedurft hätten

<u>müssen</u>   to be obliged to

INFINITIVE

PRESENT	PAST
müssen	gemusst haben

PARTICIPLES

PRESENT	PAST
	gemusst

INDICATIVE

PRESENT	PAST
muss	habe gemusst
musst	hast gemusst
muss	hat gemusst

müssen	*haben gemusst*
müsst	*habt gemusst*
müssen	*haben gemusst*

IMPERFECT	**PLUPERFECT**
musste	*hatte gemusst*
musstest	*hattest gemusst*
musste	*hatte gemusst*
mussten	*hatten gemusst*
musstet	*hattet gemusst*
mussten	*hatten gemusst*

FUTURE	**FUTURE PERFECT**
werde müssen	*werde gemusst haben*
wirst müssen	*wirst gemusst haben*
wird müssen	*wird gemusst haben*
werden müssen	*werden gemusst haben*
werdet müssen	*werdet gemusst haben*
werden müssen	*werden gemusst haben*

CONDITIONAL	**PAST CONDITIONAL**
würde müssen	*würde gemusst haben*
würdest müssen	*würdest gemusst haben*
würde müssen	*würde gemusst haben*
würden müssen	*würden gemusst haben*
würdet müssen	*würdet gemusst haben*
würden müssen	*würden gemusst haben*

SUBJUNCTIVE

PRESENT	PAST
dass ich müsse	*dass ich gemusst habe*
dass du müssest	*dass du gemusst habest*
dass er müsse	*dass er gemusst habe*
dass wir müssen	*dass wir gemusst haben*
dass ihr müsset	*dass ihr gemusst habet*
dass sie müssen	*dass sie gemusst haben*

IMPERFECT	PLUPERFECT
dass ich müsste	*dass ich gemusst hätte*
dass du müsstest	*das du gemusst hättest*
dass er müsse	*dass er gemusst hätte*
dass wir müssten	*dass wir gemusst hätten*
dass ihr müsstet	*dass ihr gemusst hättet*
dass sie müssten	*dass sie gemusst hätten*

wissen   to know

INFINITIVE

PRESENT	PAST
wissen	*gewusst haben*

PARTICIPLES

PRESENT	PAST
wissend	*gewusst*

INDICATIVE

PRESENT	PAST
weiss	*habe gewusst*
weisst	*hast gewusst*
weiss	*hat gewusst*
wissen	*haben gewusst*
wisst	*habt gewusst*
wissen	*haben gewusst*

IMPERFECT	PLUPERFECT
wusste	*hatte gewusst*
wusstest	*hattest gewusst*
wusste	*hatte gewusst*
wussten	*hatten gewusst*
wusstet	*hattet gewusst*
wussten	*hatten gewusst*

FUTURE	FUTURE PERFECT
werde wissen	*werde gewusst haben*
wirst wissen	*wirst gewusst haben*
wird wissen	*wird gewusst haben*
werden wissen	*werden gewusst haben*
werdet wissen	*werdet gewusst haben*
werden wissen	*werden gewusst haben*

CONDITIONAL	PAST CONDITIONAL
würde wissen	*würde gewusst haben*
würdest wissen	*würdest gewusst haben*
würde wissen	*würde gewusst haben*

würden wissen	*würden gewusst haben*
würdet wissen	*würdet gewusst haben*
würden wissen	*würden gewusst haben*

IMPERATIVE

wisse
wissen wir
wisst
wissen Sie

SUBJUNCTIVE

PRESENT   **PAST**

dass ich wisse	*dass ich gewusst habe*
dass du wissest	*dass du gewusst habest*
dass er wisse	*dass er gewusst habe*
dass wir wissen	*dass wir gewusst haben*
dass ihr wisset	*dass ihr gewusst habet*
dass sie wissen	*dass sie gewusst haben*

IMPERFECT   **PLUPERFECT**

dass ich wüsste	*dass ich gewusst hätte*
dass du wüsstest	*dass du gewusst hättest*
dass er wüsste	*dass er gewusst hätte*
dass wir wüssten	*dass wir gewusst hätten*
dass ihr wüsstet	*dass ihr gewusst hättet*
dass sie wüssten	*dass sie gewusst hätten*

gehen   to go

INFINITIVE

PRESENT	PAST
gehen	*gegangen sein*

PARTICIPLES

PRESENT	PAST
gehend	*gegangen*

INDICATIVE

PRESENT	PAST
gehe	*bin gegangen*
gehst	*bist gegangen*
geht	*ist gegangen*
gehen	*sind gegangen*
geht	*seid gegangen*
gehen	*sind gegangen*

IMPERFECT	PLUPERFECT
ging	*war gegangen*
gingst	*warst gegangen*
ging	*war gegangen*
gingen	*waren gegangen*
gingt	*wart gegangen*
gingen	*waren gegangen*

FUTURE	FUTURE PERFECT
werde gehen	*werde gegangen sein*
wirst gehen	*wirst gegangen sein*
wird gehen	*wird gegangen sein*
werden gehen	*werden gegangen sein*
werdet gehen	*werdet gegangen sein*
werden gehen	*werden gegangen sein*

CONDITIONAL	PAST CONDITIONAL
würde gehen	*würde gegangen sein*
würdest gehen	*würdest gegangen sein*
würde gehen	*würde gegangen sein*
würden gehen	*würden gegangen sein*
würdet gehen	*würdet gegangen sein*
würden gehen	*würden gegangen sein*

IMPERATIVE

gehe
gehen wir
geht
gehen Sie

SUBJUNCTIVE

PRESENT	PAST
dass ich gehe	*dass ich gegangen sei*
dass du gehest	*dass du gegangen seiest*
dass er gehe	*dass er gegangen sei*
dass wir gehen	*dass wir gegangen seien*
dass ihr gehet	*dass ihr gegangen seid*
dass sie gehen	*dass sie gegangen seien*

IMPERFECT	PLUPERFECT
dass ich ginge	dass ich gegangen wäre
dass du gingest	dass du gegangen wärest
dass er ginge	dass er gegangen wäre
dass wir gingen	dass wir gegangen wären
dass ihr ginget	dass ihr gegangen wäret
dass sie gingen	dass sie gegangen wären

kommen to come

INFINITIVE

PRESENT	PAST
kommen	gekommen sein

PARTICIPLES

kommend	gekommen

INDICATIVE

PRESENT	PAST
komme	bin gekommen
kommst	bist gekommen
kommt	ist gekommen
kommen	sind gekommen
kommt	seid gekommen
kommen	sind gekommen

IMPERFECT	PLUPERFECT
kam	*war gekommen*
kamst	*warst gekommen*
kam	*war gekommen*
kamen	*waren gekommen*
kamt	*wart gekommen*
kamen	*waren gekommen*

FUTURE	FUTURE PERFECT
werde kommen	*werde gekommen sein*
wirst kommen	*wirst gekommen sein*
wird kommen	*wird gekommen sein*
werden kommen	*werden gekommen sein*
werdet kommen	*werdet gekommen sein*
werden kommen	*werden gekommen sein*

CONDITIONAL	PAST CONDITIONAL
würde kommen	*würde gekommen sein*
würdest kommen	*würdest gekommen sein*
würde kommen	*würde gekommen sein*
würden kommen	*würden gekommen sein*
würdet kommen	*würdet gekommen sein*
würden kommen	*würden gekommen sein*

IMPERATIVE

komm
kommen wir
kommt
kommen Sie

SUBJUNCTIVE

PRESENT	PAST
dass ich komme	dass ich gekommen sei
dass du kommest	dass du gekommen seiest
dass er komme	dass er gekommen sei
dass wir kommen	dass wir gekommen seien
dass ihr kommet	dass ihr gekommen seid
dass sie kommen	dass sie gekommen seien

IMPERFECT	PLUPERFECT
dass ich käme	dass ich gekommen wäre
dass du kämest	dass du gekommen wärest
dass er käme	dass er gekommen wäre
dass wir kämen	dass wir gekommen wären
dass ihr kämet	dass ihr gekommen wäret
dass sie kämen	dass sie gekommen wären

40. OTHER IRREGULAR VERBS

Infinitive: *beginnen* to begin

Pres. Part.: *beginnend*

Present Indicative: *ich beginne, du beginnst, er beginnt, wir beginnen, ihr beginnt, Sie beginnen, sie beginnen.*

Present Subjunctive: *ich beginne, du beginnest, er beginne, wir beginnen, ihr beginnet, Sie beginnen, sie beginnen.*

Imperfect Indicative: *ich begann*

Imperfect Subjunctive: *Ich begänne*

Past Part.: *begonnen.*

Past Indicative: *ich habe begonnen*

Pluperfect Indicative: *ich hatte begonnen.*

Past Subjunctive: *ich hätte begonnen*

Future: *ich werde beginnen*
  ich werde begonnen haben

Conditional: *ich würde beginnen*
  ich würde begonnen haben

Imperative: *beginne, beginnen wir, beginnet, beginnen Sie*

Infinitive: *bleiben* to remain

Pres. Part.: *bleibend*

Pres. Indicative: *ich bleibe, du bleibst, er bleibt, wir bleiben, ihr bleibt, Sie bleiben, sie bleiben*

Present Subjunctive: *ich bleibe, du bliebest, er bliebe, wir bleiben, ihr bliebet, Sie bleiben, sie blieben*

Imperfect Indicative: *ich blieb*

Imperfect Subjunctive: *ich bliebe*

Past Part.: *geblieben*

Past Indicative: *ich bin geblieben*

Pluperfect Indicative: *ich war geblieben*

Past Subjunctive: *ich sei geblieben*

Pluperfect Subjunctive: *ich wäre geblieben*

Future: *ich werde bleiben*
  ich werde geblieben sein

Conditional: *ich würde bleiben*
  ich würde geblieben sein

Imperative: *bleibe, bleiben wir, bleibt, bleiben Sie*

Infinitive: _bringen_ to bring

Pres. Part.: _bringend_
Present Indicative: _ich bringe, du bringst, er bringt, wir bringen, ihr bringt, Sie bringen, sie bringen_
Present Subjunctive: _ich bringe, du bringest, er bringt, wir bringen, ihr bringet, Sie bringen, sie bringen_
Imperfect Indicative: _ich brachte_
Imperfect Subjunctive: _ich brächte_
Past Part.: _gebracht_
Past Indicative: _ich habe gebracht_
Pluperfect Indicative: _ich hatte gebracht_
Past Subjunctive: _ich habe gebracht_
Pluperfect Subjunctive: _ich hätte gebracht_
Future: _ich werde bringen_
   ich werde gebracht haben
Conditional: _ich würde bringen_
   ich würde gebracht haben
Imperative: _bringe, bringen wir, bringt, bringen Sie_

Infinitive: _denken_ to think

Pres. Part.: _denkend_
Present Indicative: _ich denke, du denkst, er denkt, wir denken, ihr denkt, Sie denken, sie denken_
Present Subjunctive: _Ich denke, du denkest, er denke, wir denken, ihr denket, Sie denken, sie denken_
Imperfect Indicative: _ich dachte_
Imperfect Subjunctive: _ich dächte_
Past. Part.: _gedacht_
Past Indicative: _ich habe gedacht_
Pluperfect Indicative: _ich hatte gedacht_
Past Subjunctive: _ich habe gedacht_
Pluperfect Subjunctive: _ich hätte gedacht_

Future: *ich werde denken*
  ich werde gedacht haben
Conditional: *ich würde denken*
  ich würde gedacht haben
Imperative: *denke, denken wir, denkt, denken Sie*

Infinitive: <u>*essen*</u> to eat

Pres. Part.: *essend*
Present Indicative: *ich esse, du isst, er isst, wir*
  essen, ihr esst, Sie essen, sie essen
Present Subjunctive: *ich esse, due essest, er esse, wir*
  essen, ihr esset, Sie essen, sie essen
Imperfect Indicative: *ich ass*
Imperfect Subjunctive: *ich ässe*
Past Part.: *gegessen*
Past Indicative: *ich habe gegessen*
Pluperfect Indicative: *ich hatte gegessen*
Past Subjunctive: *ich habe gegessen*
Pluperfect Subjunctive: *ich hätte gegessen*
Future: *ich werde essen*
  ich werde gegessen haben
Conditional: *ich würde essen*
  ich würde gegessen haben
Imperative: *iss, essen wir, esst, essen Sie*

Infinitive: <u>*fahren*</u> to drive

Pres. Part.: *fahrend*
Present Indicative: *ich fahre, du fährst, er fährt, wir*
  fahren, ihr fahrt, Sie fahren, sie fahren
Present Subjunctive: *ich fahre, du fahrest, er fahre,*
  wir fahren, ihr fahret, Sie fahren, sie fahren
Imperfect Indicative: *ich fuhr*
Imperfect Subjunctive: *ich führe*

Past. Part.: *gefahren*
Past Indicative: *ich bin gefahren*
Pluperfect Indicative: *ich war gefahren*
Past Subjunctive: *ich sei gefahren*
Pluperfect Subjunctive: *ich wäre gefahren*
Future: *ich werde fahren*
  ich werde gefahren sein
Conditional: *ich würde fahren*
  ich würde gefahren sein
Imperative: *fahre, fahren wir, fahrt, fahren Sie*

Infinitive: *fallen* to fall

Pres. Part.: *fallend*
Present Indicative: *ich falle, du fällst, er fällt, wir fallen, ihr fallt, Sie fallen, sie fallen*
Present Subjunctive: *ich falle, du fallest, er falle, wir fallen, ihr fallet, Sie fallen, sie fallen*
Imperfect Indicative: *ich fiel*
Imperfect Subjunctive: *ich fiele*
Past Part.: *gefallen*
Past Indicative: *Ich bin gefallen*
Pluperfect Indicative: *ich war gefallen*
Past Subjunctive: *ich sei gefallen*
Pluperfect Subjunctive: *ich wäre gefallen*
Future: *ich werde fallen*
  ich werde gefallen sein
Conditional: *ich würde fallen*
  ich würde gefallen sein
Imperative: *falle, fallen wir, fallt, fallen Sie*

Infinitive: *finden* to find

Pres. Part.: *findend*
Present Indicative: *ich finde, du findest, er findet, wir finden, ihr findet, Sie finden, sie finden*
Present Subjunctive: *ich finde, du findest, er finde, wir finden, ihr findet, Sie finden, sie finden*

Imperfect Indicative: *ich fand*
Imperfect Subjunctive: *ich fände*
Past Part.: *gefunden*
Past Indicative: *ich habe gefunden*
Pluperfect Indicative: *ich hatte gefunden*
Past Subjunctive: *ich habe gefunden*
Pluperfect Subjunctive: *ich hätte gefunden*
Future: *ich werde finden*
  ich werde gefunden haben
Conditional: *ich würde finden*
  ich würde gefunden haben
Imperative: *finde, finden wir, findet, finden Sie*

Infinitive: <u>*fliegen*</u> to fly

Pres. Part.: *fliegend*
Present Indicative: *ich fliege, du fliegst, er fliegt, wir
  fliegen, ihr fliegt, Sie fliegen, sie fliegen*
Present Subjunctive: *ich fliege, du fliegest, er fliege,
  wir fliegen, ihr flieget, Sie fliegen, sie fliegen*
Imperfect Indicative: *ich flog*
Imperfect Subjunctive: *ich flöge*
Past Part.: *geflogen*
Past Indicative: *ich bin geflogen*
Pluperfect Indicative: *ich war geflogen*
Past Subjunctive: *ich sei geflogen*
Pluperfect Subjunctive: *ich wäre geflogen*
Future: *ich werde fliegen*
  ich werde geflogen sein
Conditional: *ich würde fliegen*
  ich würde geflogen sein
Imperative: *fliege, fliegen wir, fliegt, fliegen Sie*

Infinitive: <u>*heissen*</u> to be called

Pres. Part.: *heissend*
Present Indicative: *ich heisse, du heisst, er heisst,
  wir heissen, ihr heisst, Sie heissen, sie heissen*

Present Subjunctive: *ich heisse, du heissest, er heisse, wir heissen, ihr heisset, Sie heissen, sie heissen*
Imperfect Indicative: *ich hiess*
Imperfect Subjunctive: *ich hiesse*
Past Part.: *geheissen*
Past Indicative: *ich habe geheissen*
Pluperfect Indicative: *ich hatte geheissen*
Past Subjunctive: *ich habe geheissen*
Pluperfect Subjunctive: *ich hätte geheissen*
Future: *ich werde heissen*
    ich werde geheissen haben
Conditional: *ich würde heissen*
    ich würde geheissen haben
Imperative: *heisse, heissen wir, heisst, heissen Sie*

Infinitive: *helfen* to help

Pres. Part.: *helfend*
Present Indicative: *ich helfe, du hilfst, er hilft, wir helfen, ihr helft, Sie helfen, sie helfen*
Present Subjunctive: *ich helfe, du helfest, er helfe, wir helfen, ihr helfet, Sie helfen, sie helfen*
Imperfect Indicative: *ich half*
Imperfect Subjunctive: *ich hälfe*
Past Part.: *geholfen*
Past Indicative: *ich habe geholfen*
Pluperfect Indicative: *ich hatte geholfen*
Past Subjunctive: *ich habe geholfen*
Pluperfect Subjunctive: *ich hätte geholfen*
Future: *ich werde helfen*
    ich werde geholfen haben
Conditional: *ich würde helfen*
    ich würde geholfen haben
Imperative: *hilf, helfen wir, helft, helfen Sie*

Infinitive: *kennen* to know

Pres. Part.: *kennend*

Present Indicative: *ich kenne, du kennst, er kennt, wir kennen, ihr kennt, Sie kennen, sie kennen*

Present Subjunctive: *ich kenne, du kennest, er kenne, wir kennen, ihr kennet, Sie kennen, sie kennen*

Imperfect Indicative: *ich kannte*

Imperfect Subjunctive: *ich kennte*

Past Part.: *gekannt*

Past Indicative: *ich habe gekannt*

Pluperfect Indicative: *ich hatte gekannt*

Past Subjunctive: *ich habe gekannt*

Pluperfect Subjunctive: *ich hätte gekannt*

Future: *ich werde kennen*
ich werde gekannt haben

Conditional: *ich würde kennen*
ich würde gekannt haben

Imperative: *kenne, kennen wir, kennt, kennen Sie*

Infinitive: <u>*laden*</u> to load

Pres. Part.: *ladend*

Present Indicative: *ich lade, du lädst, er lädt, wir laden, ihr ladet, Sie laden, sie laden*

Present Subjunctive: *Ich lade, du ladest, er lade, wir laden, ihr ladet, Sie laden, sie laden*

Imperfect Indicative: *ich lud*

Imperfect Subjunctive: *ich lüde*

Past Part.: *geladen*

Past Indicative: *ich habe geladen*

Pluperfect Indicative: *ich hatte geladen*

Past Subjunctive: *ich habe geladen*

Pluperfect Subjunctive: *ich hätte geladen*

Future: *ich werde laden*
ich werde geladen haben

Conditional: *ich würde laden*
ich würde geladen haben

Imperative: *lade, laden wir, ladet, laden Sie*

Infinitive: *lassen* to let

Pres. Part.: *lassend*
Present Indicative: *ich lasse, du lässt, er lässt, wir lassen, ihr lasst, Sie lassen, sie lassen*
Present Subjunctive: *ich lasse, du lassest, er lasse, wir lassen, ihr lasset, Sie lassen, sie lassen*
Imperfect Indicative: *ich liess*
Imperfect Subjunctive: *ich liesse*
Past Part.: *gelassen*
Past Indicative: *ich habe gelassen*
Pluperfect Indicative: *ich hatte gelassen*
Past Subjunctive: *ich habe gelassen*
Pluperfect Subjunctive: *ich hätte gelassen*
Future: *ich werde lassen*
    ich werde gelassen haben
Conditional: *ich würde lassen*
    ich würde gelassen haben
Imperative: *lass, lassen wir, lasst, lassen sie*

Infinitive: *laufen* to run

Pres. Part.: *laufend*
Present Indicative: *ich laufe, du läuft, er läuft, wir laufen, ihr lauft, Sie laufen, sie laufen*
Present Subjunctive: *ich laufe, du laufest, er laufe, wir laufen, ihr laufet, Sie laufen, sie laufen*
Imperfect Indicative: *ich lief*
Imperfect Subjunctive: *ich liefe*
Past Part.: *gelaufen*
Past Indicative: *ich bin gelaufen*
Pluperfect Indicative: *ich war gelaufen*
Past Subjunctive: *ich sei gelaufen*
Pluperfect Subjunctive: *ich wäre gelaufen*
Future: *ich werde laufen*
    ich werde gelaufen sein
Conditional: *ich würde laufen*
    ich würde gelaufen sein
Imperative: *lauf, laufen wir, lauft, laufen Sie*

Infinitive: *leiden* to suffer, endure

Pres. Part.: *leidend*
Present Indicative: *ich leide, du leidest, er leidet, wir leiden, ihr leidet, Sie leiden, sie leiden*
Present Subjunctive: *ich leide, du leidest, er leide, wir leiden, ihr leidet, Sie leiden, sie leiden*
Imperfect Indicative: *ich litt*
Imperfect Subjunctive: *ich litte*
Past Part.: *gelitten*
Past Indicative: *ich habe gelitten*
Pluperfect Indicative: *ich hatte gelitten*
Past Subjunctive: *ich habe gelitten*
Pluperfect Subjunctive: *ich hätte gelitten*
Future: *ich werde leiden*
  ich werde gelitten haben
Conditional: *ich würde leiden*
  ich würde gelitten haben
Imperative: *leide, leiden, wir, leidet, leiden Sie*

Infinitive: *lesen* to read

Pres. Part.: *lesend*
Present Indicative; *ich lese, du liest, er liest, wir lesen, ihr lest, Sie lesen, sie lesen*
Present Subjunctive: *ich lese, du lesest, er lese, wir lesen, ihr leset, Sie lesen, sie lesen*
Imperfect Indicative: *ich las*
Imperfect Subjunctive: *ich läse*
Past Part.: *gelesen*
Past Indicative: *ich habe gelesen*
Pluperfect Indicative: *ich hatte gelesen*
Past Subjunctive: *ich habe gelesen*
Pluperfect Subjunctive: *ich hätte gelesen*
Future: *ich werde lesen*
  ich werde gelesen haben
Conditional: *ich würde lesen*
  ich würde gelesen haben
Imperative: *lies, lesen wir, lest, lesen Sie*

Infinitive: *liegen* to lie (recline)

Pres. Part.: *liegend*

Present Indicative: *ich liege, du liegst, er liegt, wir liegen, ihr liegt, Sie liegen, sie liegen*

Present Subjunctive: *ich liege, du liegest, er liege, wir liegen, ihr lieget, Sie liegen, sie liegen*

Imperfect Indicative: *ich lag*

Imperfect Subjunctive: *ich läge*

Past Part.: *gelegen*

Past Indicative: *ich habe gelegen*

Past Subjunctive: *ich hätte gelegen*

Future: *ich werde liegen*
   ich werde gelegen haben

Conditional: *ich würde liegen*
   ich würde gelegen haben

Imperative: *liege, liegen wir, liegt, liegen Sie*

Infinitive: *lügen* to lie (say something untrue)

Pres. Part.: *lügend*

Present Indicative: *ich lüge, du lügst, er lügt, wir lügen, ihr lügt, Sie lügen, sie lügen*

Present Subjunctive: *ich lüge, du lügest, er lüge, wir lügen, ihr lüget, Sie lügen, sie lügen*

Imperfect Indicative: *ich log*

Imperfect Subjunctive: *ich löge*

Past Part.: *gelogen*

Past Indicative: *ich habe gelogen*

Pluperfect Indicative: *ich hatte gelogen*

Past Subjunctive: *ich habe gelogen*

Pluperfect Subjunctive: *ich hätte gelogen*

Future: *ich werde lügen*
   ich werde gelogen haben

Conditional: *ich würde lugen*
   ich würde gelogen haben

Imperative: *lüge, lügen wir, lügt, lügen Sie*

Infinitive: *nehmen* to take

Pres. Part.: *nehmend*

Present Indicative: *ich nehme, du nimmst, er nimmt, wir nehmen, ihr nehmt, Sie nehmen, sie nehmen*
Present Subjunctive: *ich nehme, du nehmest, er nehme, wir nehmen, ihr nehmet, Sie nehmen, sie nehmen*
Imperfect Indicative: *ich nahm*
Imperfect Subjunctive: *ich nähme*
Past Part.: *genommen*
Past Indicative: *ich habe genommen*
Pluperfect Indicative: *ich hatte genommen*
Past Subjunctive: *ich habe genommen*
Pluperfect Subjunctive: *ich hätte genommen*
Future: *ich werde nehmen*
ich werde genommen haben
Conditional: *ich würde nehmen*
ich würde genommen haben
Imperative: *nimm, nehmen wir, nehmt, nehmen Sie*

Infinitive: *nennen* to name

Pres. Part.: *nennend*
Present Indicative: *ich nenne, du nennst, er nennt, wir nennen, ihr nennt, Sie nennen, sie nennen*
Present Subjunctive: *ich nenne, du nennest, er nenne, wir nennen, ihr nennet, Sie nennen, sie nennen*
Imperfect Indicative: *ich nannte*
Imperfect Subjunctive: *ich nennte*
Past Part.: *genannt*
Past Indicative: *ich habe genannt*
Pluperfect Indicative: *ich hatte genannt*
Past Subjunctive: *ich habe genannt*
Pluperfect Subjunctive: *ich hätte genannt*
Future: *ich werde nennen*
ich werde genannt haben
Conditional: *ich würde nennen*
ich würde genannt haben

Imperative: *nenne, nennen wir, nennt, nennen Sie*

Infinitive: *rufen* to call

Pres. Part.: *rufend*

Present Indicative: *ich rufe, du rufst, er ruft, wir rufen, ihr ruft, Sie rufen, sie rufen*

Present Subjunctive: *ich rufe, du rufest, er rufe, wir rufen, rufet, Sie rufen, sie rufen*

Imperfect Indicative: *ich rief*

Imperfect Subjunctive: *ich riefe*

Past Part.: *gerufen*

Past Indicative: *ich habe gerufen*

Pluperfect Indicative: *ich hatte gerufen*

Past Subjunctive: *ich habe gerufen*

Pluperfect Subjunctive: *ich hätte gerufen*

Future: *ich werde rufen*
  ich werde gerufen haben

Conditional: *ich würde rufen*
  ich würde gerufen haben

Imperative: *rufe, rufen wir, ruft, rufen Sie*

Infinitive: *schaffen* to create

Pres. Part.: *schaffend*

Present Indicative: *ich schaffe, du schaffst, er schafft, wir schaffen, ihr schafft, Sie schaffen, sie schaffen*

Present Subjunctive: *ich schaffe, du schaffest, er schaffe, wir schaffen, ihr schaffet, Sie schaffen, sie schaffen*

Imperfect Indicative: *ich schuf*

Imperfect Subjunctive: *ich schufe*

Past Part.: *geschaffen*

Past Indicative: *ich habe geschaffen*

Pluperfect Indicative: *ich hatte geschaffen*

Past Subjunctive: *ich habe geschaffen*

Pluperfect Subjunctive: *ich hätte geschaffen*

Future: *ich werde schaffen*
  ich werde geschaffen haben

Conditional: *ich würde schaffen*
ich würde geschaffen haben
Imperative: *schaffe, schaffen wir, schafft, schaffen Sie*

Infinitive: *schlafen* to sleep

Pres. Part.: *schlafend*
Present Indicative: *ich schlafe, du schläfst, er schläft, wir schlafen, ihr schlaft, sie schlafen*
Present Subjunctive: *ich schlafe, du schlafest, er schlafe, wir schlafen, ihr schlafet, sie schlafen*
Imperfect Indicative: *ich schlief*
Imperfect Subjunctive: *ich schliefe*
Past Part.: *geschlafen*
Past Indicative: *ich habe geschlafen*
Pluperfect Indicative: *Ich hatte geschlafen*
Past Subjunctive: *ich habe geschlafen*
Pluperfect Subjunctive: *ich hätte geschlafen*
Future: *ich werde schlafen*
ich werde geschlafen haben
Conditional: *ich würde schlafen*
ich würde geschlafen haben
Imperative: *schlafe, schlafen wir, schlaft, schlafen Sie*

Infinitive: *schlagen* to beat, to strike

Pres. Part.: *schlagend*
Present Indicative: *ich schlage, du schlägst, er schlägt, wir schlagen, ihr schlagt, Sie schlagen, sie schlagen*
Present Subjunctive: *ich schlage, du schlagest, er schlage, wir schlagen, ihr schlaget, Sie schlagen, sie schlagen*
Imperfect Indicative: *ich schlug*
Imperfect Subjunctive: *ich schlüge*
Past Part.: *geschlagen*
Past Indicative: *ich habe geschlagen*
Pluperfect Indicative: *ich hatte geschlagen*

Past Subjunctive: *ich habe geschlagen*
Pluperfect Subjunctive: *ich hätte geschlagen*
Future: *ich werde schlagen*
  ich werde geschlagen haben
Conditional: *ich würde schlagen*
  ich würde geschlagen haben
Imperative: *schlage, schlagen wir, schlagt, schlagen Sie*

Infinitive: <u>*schreiben*</u> to write

Pres. Part.: *schreibend*
Present Indicative: *ich schreibe, du schreibst, er schreibt, wir schreiben, ihr schreibt, Sie schreiben, sie schreiben*
Present Subjunctive: *ich schreibe, du schreibest, er schreibe, wir schreiben, ihr schreibet, Sie schreiben, sie schreiben*
Imperfect Indicative: *ich schrieb*
Imperfect Subjunctive: *ich schriebe*
Past Part.: *geschrieben*
Past Indicative: *ich habe geschrieben*
Pluperfect Indicative: *ich hatte geschrieben*
Past Subjunctive: *ich habe geschrieben*
Pluperfect Subjunctive: *ich hätte geschrieben*
Future: *ich werde schreiben*
  ich werde geschrieben haben
Conditional: *ich würde schreiben*
  ich würde geschrieben haben
Imperative: *schreibe, schreiben wir, schreibt, schreiben Sie*

Infinitive: <u>*schmelzen*</u> to melt

Pres. Part.: *schmelzend*
Present Indicative: *ich schmelze, du schmilzt, er schmilzt, wir schmelzen, ihr schmelzt, Sie schmelzen, sie schmelzen*

Present Subjunctive: *ich schmelze, du schmelzest, er schmelze, wir schmelzen, ihr schmelzet, Sie schmelzen, sie schmelzen*

Imperfect Indicative: *ich schmolz*

Imperfect Subjunctive: *ich schmölze*

Past Part.: *geschmolzen*

Past Indicative: *ich bin geschmolzen*

Pluperfect Indicative: *ich war geschmolzen*

Past Subjunctive: *ich sei geschmolzen*

Pluperfect Subjunctive: *ich wäre geschmolzen*

Future: *ich werde schmelzen*
ich werde geschmolzen sein

Conditional: *ich würde schmelzen*
ich würde geschmolzen sein

Imperative: *schmilz, schmelzen wir, schmelzt, schmelzen Sie*

Infinitive: *schwimmen* to swim

Pres. Part.: *schwimmend*

Present Indicative: *ich schwimme, du schwimmst, er schwimmt, wir schwimmen, ihr schwimmt, Sie schwimmen, sie schwimmen*

Present Subjunctive: *ich schwimme, du schwimmest, er schwimme, wir schwimmen, ihr schwimmet, Sie schwimmen, sie schwimmen*

Imperfect Indicative: *ich schwamm*

Imperfect Subjunctive: *ich schwämme*

Past Part.: *geschwommen*

Past Indicative: *ich bin geschwommen*

Pluperfect Indicative: *ich war geschwommen*

Past Subjunctive: *ich sei geschwommen*

Pluperfect Subjunctive: *ich wäre geschwommen*

Future: *ich werde schwimmen*
ich werde geschwommen sein

Conditional: *ich würde schwimmen*
ich würde geschwommen sein

Imperative: *schwimme, schwimmen wir, schwimmt, schwimmen Sie*

Infinitive: *senden* to send

Pres. Part.: *sendend*
Present Indicative: *ich sende, du sendest, er sendet, wir senden, ihr sendet, Sie senden, sie senden*
Present Subjunctive: *ich sende, du sendest, er sendet, wir senden, ihr sendet, Sie senden, sie senden*
Imperfect Indicative: *ich sandte* (or *sendete*)
Imperfect Subjunctive: *ich sändete*
Past Part.: *gesandt*
Past Indicative: *ich habe gesandt*
Pluperfect Indicative: *ich hatte gesandt*
Pluperfect Subjunctive: *ich hätte gesandt*
Future: *ich werde senden*
  ich werde gesandt haben
Conditional: *ich würde senden*
  ich würde gesandt haben
Imperative: *sende, senden wir, sendet, senden Sie*

Infinitive: *singen* to sing

Pres. Part.: *singend*
Present Indicative: *ich singe, du singst, er singt, wir singen, ihr singt, Sie singen, sie singen*
Present Subjunctive: *ich singe, du singest, er singe, wir singen, ihr singet, Sie singen, sie singen*
Imperfect Indicative: *ich sang*
Imperfect Subjunctive: *ich sänge*
Past Part.: *gesungen*
Past Indicative: *ich habe gesungen*
Pluperfect Indicative: *ich hatte gesungen*
Past Subjunctive: *ich habe gesungen*
Pluperfect Subjunctive: *ich hätte gesungen*
Future: *ich werde singen*
  ich werde gesungen haben
Conditional: *ich würde singen*
  ich würde gesungen haben
Imperative: *singe, singen wir, singt, singen Sie*

Infinitive: *sitzen* to sit

Pres. Part.: *sitzend*
Present Indicative: *ich sitze, du sitzt, er sitzt, wir sitzen, ihr sitzt, Sie sitzen, sie sitzen*
Present Subjunctive: *ich sitze, du sitzest, er sitze, wir sitzen, ihr sitzet, Sie sitzen, sie sitzen*
Imperfect Indicative: *ich sass*
Imperfect Subjunctive: *ich sässe*
Past Part.: *gesessen*
Past Indicative: *ich habe gesessen*
Pluperfect Indicative: *ich hatte gesessen*
Past Subjunctive: *ich habe gesessen*
Pluperfect Subjunctive: *ich hätte gesessen*
Future: *ich werde sitzen*
 ich werde gesessen haben
Conditional: *ich würde sitzen*
 ich würde gesessen haben
Imperative: *sitze, sitzen wir, sitzt, sitzen Sie*

Infinitive: *stehen* to stand

Pres. Part.: *stehend*
Pres. Indicative: *ich stehe, du stehst, er steht, wir stehen, ihr steht, Sie stehen, sie stehen*
Present Subjunctive: *ich stehe, du stehest, er stehe, wir stehen, ihr stehet, Sie stehen, sie stehen*
Imperfect Indicative: *ich stand*
Imperfect Subjunctive: *ich stände*
Past Part.: *gestanden*
Past Indicative: *ich habe gestanden*
Pluperfect Indicative: *ich hatte gestanden*
Past Subjunctive: *ich habe gestanden*
Pluperfect Subjunctive: *ich hätte gestanden*
Future: *ich werde stehen*
 ich werde gestanden haben
Conditional: *ich würde stehen*
 ich würde gestanden haben
Imperative: *stehe, stehen wir, steht, stehen Sie*

Infinitive: *stehlen* to steal

Pres. Part.: *stehlend*
Present Indicative: *ich stehle, du stiehlst, er stiehlt,
wir stehlen, ihr stehlt, Sie stehlen, sie stehlen*
Present Subjunctive: *ich stehle, du stehlest, er stehle,
wir stehlen, ihr stehlet, Sie stehlen, sie stehlen*
Imperfect Indicative: *ich stahl*
Imperfect Subjunctive: *ich stähle*
Past Part.: *gestohlen*
Past Indicative: *ich habe gestohlen*
Pluperfect Indicative: *ich hatte gestohlen*
Past Subjunctive: *ich habe gestohlen*
Pluperfect Subjunctive: *ich hätte gestohlen*
Future: *ich werde stehlen
ich werde gestohlen haben*
Conditional: *ich würde stehlen
ich würde gestohlen haben*
Imperative: *stiehl, stehlen wir, stehlt, stehlen Sie*

Infinitive: *springen* to jump

Pres. Part.: *springend*
Present Indicative: *ich springe, du springst, er
springt, wir springen, ihr springt, Sie springen, sie
springen*
Present Subjunctive: *ich springe, du springest, er
springe, wir springen, ihr springet, Sie springen,
sie springen*
Imperfect Indicative: *ich sprang*
Imperfect Subjunctive: *ich spränge*
Past Part.: *gesprungen*
Past Indicative: *ich bin gesprungen*
Pluperfect Indicative: *ich war gesprungen*
Past Subjunctive: *ich sei gesprungen*
Pluperfect Subjunctive: *ich wäre gesprungen*
Future: *ich werde springen
ich werde gesprungen sein*

Conditional: *ich würde springen*
  ich würde gesprungen sein
Imperative: *spring, springen wir, springt, springen
  Sie*

Infinitive: *tragen* to carry

Pres. Part.: *tragend*
Present Indicative: *ich trage, du trägst, er trägt, wir
  tragen, ihr tragt, Sie tragen, sie tragen*
Present Subjunctive: *ich trage, du tragest, er trage,
  wir tragen, ihr traget, Sie tragen, sie tragen*
Imperfect Indicative: *ich trug*
Imperfect Subjunctive: *ich trüge*
Past Part.: *getragen*
Past Indicative: *ich habe getragen*
Pluperfect Indicative: *ich hatte getragen*
Past Subjunctive: *ich habe getragen*
Pluperfect Subjunctive: *ich hätte getragen*
Future: *ich werde tragen*
  ich werde getragen haben
Conditional: *ich würde tragen*
  ich würde getragen haben
Imperative: *trage, tragen wir, tragt, tragen Sie*

Infinitive: *treffen* to meet

Pres. Part.: *treffend*
Present Indicative: *ich treffe, du triffst, er trifft, wir
  treffen, ihr trefft, Sie treffen, sie treffen*
Present Subjunctive: *ich treffe, du treffest, er treffe,
  wir treffen, ihr treffet, Sie treffen, sie treffen*
Imperfect Indicative: *ich traf*
Imperfect Subjunctive: *ich träfe*
Past Part.: *getroffen*
Past Indicative: *ich habe getroffen*
Pluperfect Indicative: *ich hätte getroffen*
Past Subjunctive: *ich habe getroffen*
Pluperfect Subjunctive: *ich hätte getroffen*

Future: *ich werde treffen*
 ich werde getroffen haben
Conditional: *ich würde treffen*
 ich würde getroffen haben
Imperative: *triff, treffen wir, trefft, treffen Sie*

Infinitive: *trinken* to drink

Pres. Part.: *trinkend*
Present Indicative: *ich trinke, du trinkst, er trinkt,*
 wir trinken, ihr trinkt, Sie trinken, sie trinken
Present Subjunctive: *ich trinke, du trinkest, er trinke,*
 wir trinken, ihr trinket, Sie trinken, sie trinken
Imperfect Indicative: *ich trank*
Imperfect Subjunctive: *ich tränke*
Past Part.: *getrunken*
Past Indicative: *ich habe getrunken*
Pluperfect Indicative: *ich hatte getrunken*
Past Subjunctive: *ich habe getrunken*
Pluperfect Subjunctive: *ich hätte getrunken*
Future: *ich werde trinken*
 ich werde getrunken haben
Conditional: *ich würde trinken*
 ich würde getrunken haben
Imperative: *trink, trinken wir, trinkt, trinken Sie*

Infinitive: *tun* to do

Pres. Part.: *tuend*
Present Indicative: *ich tue, du tust, er tut, wir tun,*
 ihr tut, Sie tun, sie tun
Present Subjunctive: *ich tue, du tuest, er tue, wir*
 tun, ihr tuet, Sie tun, sie tun
Imperfect Indicative: *ich tat*
Imperfect Subjunctive: *ich täte*
Past Part.: *getan*

Past Indicative: *ich habe getan*
Pluperfect Indicative: *ich hatte getan*
Past Subjunctive: *ich habe getan*
Pluperfect Subjunctive: *ich hätte getan*
Future: *ich werde tun*
  ich werde getan haben
Conditional: *ich würde tun*
  ich würde getan haben
Imperative: *tue, tun wir, tut, tun Sie*

Infinitive: *vergessen* to forget

Pres. Part.: *vergessend*
Present Indicative: *ich vergesse, du vergisst, er vergisst, wir vergessen, ihr vergesst, Sie vergessen, sie vergessen*
Present Subjunctive: *ich vergesse, du vergessest, er vergesse, wir vergessen, ihr vergesset, Sie vergessen, sie vergessen*
Imperfect Indicative: *ich vergass*
Imperfect Subjunctive: *ich vergässe*
Past Part.: *vergessen*
Past Indicative: *ich habe vergessen*
Pluperfect Indicative: *ich hatte vergessen*
Past Subjunctive: *ich habe vergessen*
Pluperfect Subjunctive: *ich hätte vergessen*
Future: *ich werde vergessen*
  ich werde vergessen haben
Conditional: *ich würde vergessen*
  ich würde vergessen haben
Imperative: *vergiss, vergessen wir, vergesst, vergessen Sie*

Infinitive: *verlieren* to lose

Pres. Part.: *verlierend*
Present Indicative: *ich verliere, du verlierst, er verliert, wir verlieren, ihr verliert, Sie verlieren, sie verlieren*

Present Subjunctive: *ich verliere, du verlierest, er verliere, wir verlieren, ihr verlieret, Sie verlieren, sie verlieren*

Imperfect Indicative: *ich verlor*

Imperfect Subjunctive: *ich verlöre*

Past Part.: *verloren*

Past Indicative: *ich habe verloren*

Pluperfect Indicative: *ich hatte verloren*

Past Subjunctive: *ich habe verloren*

Pluperfect Subjunctive: *ich hätte verloren*

Future: *ich werde verlieren*
ich werde verloren haben

Conditional: *ich würde verlieren*
ich würde verloren haben

Imperative: *verliere, verlieren wir, verliert, verlieren Sie*

LETTER WRITING
1. THANK-YOU NOTES

Berlin, den 14. März 1985

Sehr geehrte Frau Zimmermann,
Ich möchte Ihnen herzlich für Ihr wundervolles Geschenk danken. Das Bild entspricht ganz meinem Geschmack und passt so gut zu den andern Dingen in meinem Wohnzimmer.
Meinen allerherzlichsten Dank.

Mit verbindlichen Grüssen

Lotte Schäfer

Berlin, March 14, 1985

Dear Mrs. Zimmermann,
   I should like to thank you for your delightful
present. The picture is entirely to my taste and
matches the other things in my living-room
perfectly.
   Thank you ever so much.

Sincerely yours,

Lotte Schäfer

2. BUSINESS LETTERS

H. Molz
Berlin
Kantstrasse 16
Berlin, den 2. Mai 1985

Verlag Peter Basten
Berlin
Kurfürstendamm 10

   *In der Anlage übersende ich Ihnen einen Scheck
über DM 23.—für ein Jahresabonnement Ihrer
Zeitschrift.*

Hochachtungsvoll!

Heinrich Molz

ANLAGE

H. Mulz
16 Kant Street
Berlin
May 2, 1985

Peter Basten Press
10 Kurfurstendamm
Berlin

Gentlemen:

Enclosed please find a check for 23 marks for a
year's subscription to your magazine.

Very truly yours,

Heinrich Molz

(Encl.)

Schwarzkopf & Co.
Berlin
Breite Strasse 6
Berlin, den 30. September
1985

Firma
Paul Gerber & Co
Berlin
van Groothestrasse 20

In Beantwortung Ihrer Anfrage vom 10. ds.
bestätigen wir Ihnen gerne nochmals die Aufgabe
der Sendung per Postpaket am 13. August.

Hochachtungsvoll

Ernst Schwarzkopf

6 Broad Street
Berlin
September 30, 1985

Paul Gerber & Co.
20 van Groothe Street
Berlin

Gentlemen:

In reply to your letter ("inquiry") of this month,
we wish to confirm once more that the merchandise
was mailed to you parcel post on August 13.

Very truly yours,

Ernst Schwarzkopf

3. INFORMAL LETTERS

5. März 1985

Lieber Jakob,
Ich habe mich sehr über Deinen letzten Brief
gefreut.
Zunächst habe ich eine gute Nachricht für Dich.
Anfang April beabsichtige ich, zwei Wochen in
Berlin zu verbringen. Ich sehe mit Freude einem
Wiedersehen mit Dir und Deiner Familie entgegen
und ich hoffe dass es Euch alle gut geht.
Irene kommt mit mir; sie freut sich sehr, nun
endlich Deine Frau kennenzulernen. Auf diese Weise
wird es uns gelingen, die beiden Frauen plaudern zu
lassen, und wir können uns den ganzen Nachmittag
unterhalten, so wie wir es in der Schule immer getan
haben. Das Geschäft geht ganz gut zur Zeit. Hoffen
wir, dass es so bleibt. Versuche, nicht zuviele
Patienten während des Monats April anzunehmen,

*obwohl ich glaube, dass es etwas schwierig sein
wird.*

*Neulich fragte Müller nach Dir. Sein Geschäft
geht gut.*

*Fast hätte ich die Hauptsache vergessen. Kannst
Du mir ein Zimmer im Grand Hotel für den fünften
April reservieren? Du tätest mir einen grossen
Gefallen.*

*Ich hoffe bald von Dir zu hören. Meine besten
Grüsse an Deine Frau.*

Dein

Klaus

March 5, 1985

Dear Jack,

I was very happy to receive your last letter.

First of all, I've some good news for you. I expect
to spend two weeks in Berlin at the beginning of
April and I'm looking forward to the prospect of
seeing you and your family, all of whom I hope are
well.

Irene's coming with me; she's delighted to be able
at last to meet your wife. That way we shall be able
to let our two wives talk and we can spend the
afternoon talking together as we used to at school.
Business is pretty good right now. Let's hope it will
keep up. Try not to get too many patients during the
month of April, though I suppose that's a little
difficult to arrange.

The other day Müller asked about you. His
business is going well.

I almost forgot the most important thing. Can you
reserve a room for me at the Grand Hotel for April
fifth? You'll be doing me a great favor.

I hope to hear from you soon. My best regards to your wife.

Yours,

Nicolas

4. FORMS OF SALUTATIONS AND COMPLIMENTARY CLOSINGS

SALUTATIONS:

FORMAL

Sehr geehrter Herr Professor,	Dear Professor (Smith)
Sehr geehrter Herr Bürgermeister,	Dear Mayor (Smith)
Sehr geehrter Herr Rechtsanwalt, Sehr geehrter Herr Doktor,	Dear Mr. (Smith): (Lawyers are often addressed as "Doktor" in Germany.)
Sehr geehrte Herren,	Gentlemen:
Sehr geehrter Herr Schneider,	Dear Mr. Schneider:

INFORMAL

Mein lieber Karl,	Dear Karl,
Meine liebe Franziska,	Dear Frances,
Mein Liebling,	My darling (*m.* and *f.*)
Mein Liebster,	My darling (*m.*)
Meine Liebste,	My darling (*f.*)
Lieber Franz,	Dear Frank,
Liebe Paula,	Dear Paula,

COMPLIMENTARY CLOSINGS:

FORMAL

1. *Hochachtungsvoll!* ("Full of high respect") — Very truly yours

2. *Mit vorzüglicher*   Very truly yours
   Hochachtung!
   ("With the most excellent and highest
   regard")
3. *Mit besten Grüssen,*   Yours truly
   ("With best greetings")
4. *Wir empfehlen uns,*   Yours truly
   mit besten Grüssen,
   ("We commend ourselves with best regards")

INFORMAL

1. *Mit herzlichem*   Very sincerely
   Gruss
   ("With hearty greeting")
2. *Bitte grüsse Deine*   Please give my regards
   Mutter von mir   to your mother
3. *Meine besten Grüsse*   Give my regards to
   an die Deinen   your family
4. *Grüsse und Küsse*   My love to everybody
   an Euch alle
   ("greetings and kisses to you all")
5. *Mit herzlichem*   Love
   Gruss

5. FORM OF THE ENVELOPE

Schwarzkopf & Co.
Berlin-Neuköln
Breite Strasse 6

Firma
Schiller & Kramer
Berlin
Kurfürstendamm 75

Letters to an individual are addressed:

Herr   H. Muller   (Mr.)
Frau   F. Schneider   (Mrs.)
Fraulein   Frl. Kurz   (Miss)